Read-Aloud Poems

Read-Aloud
Poems

EDITED BY

GLORYA HALE

BLACK DOG
& LEVENTHAL
PUBLISHERS
NEW YORK

Published by
Black Dog & Leventhal Publishers, Inc.
151 West 19th Street New York, NY 10011

Distributed by
Workman Publishing Company
225 Varick Street New York, NY 10014

"Life Doesn't Frighten Me", copyright © 1978 by Maya Angelou, from
AND STILL I RISE by Maya Angelou used by permission of Random House, Inc.
"Caged Bird", copyright © 1983 by Maya Angelou, from SHAKER, WHY DON'T YOU SING? by
Maya Angelou. Used by permission of Random House, Inc.

Manufactured in Malaysia
Cover and interior design by Liz Driesbach
Cover illustration by Lisa Falkenstern

ISBN: 978-1-57912-921-7

h g f e d c b a

Library of Congress Cataloging-in-Publication Data available on file.

Contents

———

NATURE'S PEOPLE

MEET THE FAMILY

JUST ME

FRIENDSHIP AND LOVE

LAUGHING LYRICS

EARTH AND SKY

POEMS THAT TELL STORIES

LET'S PRETEND

POEMS TO PONDER

NATURE'S PEOPLE

In Emily Dickenson's poem "The Snake," she refers to "nature's people."
In this section you will make the acquaintance of many of nature's
people including kittens and dogs, a sloth and a camel, a tiger and
a crocodile, and, of course, Emily Dickenson's snake.

The Cow

The friendly cow all red and white,
    I love with all my heart:
She gives me cream with all her might,
    To eat with apple tart.

She wanders lowing here and there,
    And yet she cannot stray,
All in the pleasant open air,
    The pleasant light of day;

And blown by all the winds that pass
    And wet with all the showers,
She walks among the meadow grass
    And eats the meadow flowers.

–ROBERT LOUIS STEVENSON

Many of Robert Louis Stevenson's poems are included in this book. Most of them come from his collection of poems– *A Child's Garden of Verses*. Stevenson also wrote travel books and such famous novels as *Treasure Island* and *Dr. Jekyll and Mr. Hyde*.

Choosing
Their Names

Our old cat has kittens three—
What do you think their names should be?
One is tabby with emerald eyes,
      And a tail that's long and slender,
And into a temper she quickly flies
      If you ever by chance offend her.
      I think we shall call her this—
          I think we shall call her that—
Now, don't you think that Pepperpot
      Is a nice name for a cat?

One is black with a frill of white,
      And her feet are all white fur,
If you stroke her she carries her tail upright
      And quickly begins to purr.
      I think we shall call her this—
          I think we shall call her that—
Now, don't you think that Sootikin
      Is a nice name for a cat?

One is a tortoiseshell yellow and black,
      With plenty of white about him;
If you tease him, at once he sets up his back,
      He's a quarrelsome one, ne'er doubt him.
      I think we shall call him this—
          I think we shall call him that—
Now, don't you think that Scratchaway
      Is a nice name for a cat?

Our old cat has kittens three
And I fancy these their names will be:
Pepperpot, Sootikin, Scratchaway—there!
Were ever kittens with these to compare?
And we call the old mother—
        Now, what do you think?
Tabitha Longclaws Tiddley Wink.

—THOMAS HOOD

The Lion

When Lion sends his roaring forth,
Silence falls upon the earth;
For the creatures, great and small,
Know his terror-breathing call;
And, as if by death pursued,
Leave him to a solitude.

Lion, thou art made to dwell
In hot lands, intractable,
And thyself, the sun, the sand,
Are a tyrannous triple band;
Lion-king and desert throne,
All the region is your own!

—MARY HOWETT

The Kitten
at Play

See the kitten on the wall,
Sporting with the leaves that fall,
Withered leaves, one, two, and three
Falling from the elder tree,
Through the calm and frosty air
Of the morning bright and fair.

See the kitten, how she starts,
Crouches, stretches, paws, and darts
With a tiger-leap half way
Now she meets her coming prey.
Lets it go as fast and then
Has it in her power again.

Now she works with three and four,
Like an Indian conjurer;
Quick as he in feats of art,
Gracefully she plays her part;
Yet were gazing thousands there,
What would little Tabby care?

—WILLIAM WORDSWORTH

Lone Dog

I'm a lean dog, a keen dog, a wild dog, and lone;
I'm a rough dog, a tough dog, hunting on my own;
I'm a bad dog, a mad dog, teasing silly sheep;
I love to sit and bay the moon, to keep fat souls from sleep.

I'll never be a lap dog, licking dirty feet,
A sleek dog, a meek dog, cringing for my meat,
Not for me the fireside, the well-filled plate,
But shut door, and sharp stone, and cuff and kick and hate.

Not for me the other dogs, running by my side,
Some have run a short while, but none of them would bide,
Oh, mine is still the lone trail, the hard trail, the best,
Wide wind, and wild stars, and hunger of the quest!

—IRENE RUTHERFORD McLEOD

The Robin

The robin is the one
That interrupts the morn
With hurried, few, express reports
When March is scarcely on.

The robin is the one
That overflows the noon
With her cherubic quantity,
As April has begun.

The robin is the one
That speechless from her nest
Submits that home and certainty
And sanctity are best.

—EMILY DICKINSON

Emily Dickinson, one
of America's great
poets, spent almost her
entire life in Amherst,
Massachusetts. Only six
poems were published
during her lifetime, but
after she died more
than a thousand were
found in manuscript.
Some of them are
included in this book.

The Fly

Little fly,
Thy summer's play
My thoughtless hand
Has brush'd away.

Am not I
A fly like thee?
Or art not thou
A man like me?

For I dance,
And drink, & sing;
Till some blind hand
Shall brush my wing.

If thought is life
And strength & breath,
And the want
Of thought is death;

Then am I
A happy fly,
If I live
Or if I die.

—WILLIAM BLAKE

Fireflies

Little lamps of the dusk,
       You fly low and gold
When the summer evening
       Starts to unfold.
So that all the insects,
       Now, before you pass,
Will have light to see by,
       Undressing in the grass.

But when the night has flowered,
       Little lamps agleam,
You fly over treetops
       Following a dream.
Men wonder from their windows
       That a firefly goes so far—
They do not know your longing
       To be a shooting star.

–CAROLYN HALL

The Tiger

Tiger! Tiger! burning bright,
In the forests of the night,
What immortal hand or eye
Could frame thy fearful symmetry?

In what distant deeps or skies
Burnt the fire of thine eyes?
On what wings dare he aspire?
What the hand dare seize the fire?

And what shoulder, and what art,
Could twist the sinews of thy heart?
And when thy heart began to beat,
What dread hand and what dread feet?

What the hammer? what the chain?
In what furnace was thy brain?
What the anvil? what dread grasp
Dare its deadly terrors clasp?

When the stars threw down their spears,
And watered heaven with their tears,
Did He smile His work to see?
Did He who made the Lamb, make thee?

Tiger! Tiger! burning bright,
In the forests of the night,
What immortal hand or eye
Dare frame thy fearful symmetry?

—WILLIAM BLAKE

William Blake was born in London in 1757 and lived there all his life. In addition to being a poet, he was an artist and an engraver. This poem was included in his book *Songs of Experience*; it was hand-lettered and illustrated with Blake's drawing of a tiger prowling through the jungle.

The Sandpiper

Across the lonely beach we flit,
     One little sandpiper and I;
And fast I gather, bit by bit,
     The scattered driftwood, bleached and dry.
The wild waves reach their hands for it,
     The wild wind raves, the tide runs high,
As up and down the beach we flit—
     One little sandpiper and I.

Above our heads the sullen clouds
     Scud black and swift across the sky;
Like silent ghosts in misty shrouds
     Stand out the white lighthouses high.
Almost as far as eye can reach
     I see the close-reefed vessels fly,
As fast we flit along the beach—
     One little sandpiper and I.

I watch him as he skims along
     Uttering his sweet and mournful cry;
He starts not at my fitful song
     Or flash of fluttering drapery.
He has no thought of any wrong,
     He scans me with a fearless eye;
Staunch friends are we, well-tried and strong,
     The little sandpiper and I.

Comrade, where wilt thou be tonight
     When the loosed storm breaks furiously?

Celia Thaxter grew up on the Isles of Shoals, off the coast of New Hampshire, where her father was the lighthouse keeper. In the nineteenth century she was one of the best known women poets. She wrote for adults as well as for children. "The Sandpiper" is one of her most popular poems.

My driftwood fire will burn so bright!
      To what warm shelter canst thou fly?
I do not feel for thee, though wroth
      The tempest rushes through the sky:
For are we not God's children both,
      Thou, little sandpiper, and I?

—CELIA THAXTER

The Camel's Complaint

Canary birds feed on sugar and seed,
      Parrots have crackers to crunch;
And as for the poodles, they tell me the noodles
      Have chicken and cream for their lunch.
            But there's never a question
            About my digestion—
                Anything does for me.

Cats, you're aware, can repose in a chair,
      Chickens can roost upon rails;
Puppies are able to sleep in a stable,
      And oysters can slumber in pails.
            But no one supposes
            A poor camel dozes—
                Any place does for me.

Lambs are enclosed where it's never exposed,
      Coops are constructed for hens;

Kittens are treated to houses well heated,
          And pigs are protected by pens.
                    But a camel comes handy
                    Wherever it's sandy—
                              Anywhere does for me.

People would laugh if you rode a giraffe,
          Or mounted the back of an ox;
It's nobody's habit to ride on a rabbit,
          Or try to bestraddle a fox.
                    But as for a camel, he's
                    Ridden by families—
                              Any load does for me.

A snake is as round as a hole in the ground,
          And weasels are wavy and sleek;
And no alligator could ever be straighter
          Than lizards that live in a creek.
                    But a camel's all lumpy
                    And bumpy and humpy—
                              Any shape does for me.

—CHARLES E. CARRYL

Charles E. Carryl,
an American, was a
member of the New
York Stock exchange.
He wrote novels for
children, which appeared
in installments in the
magazine St. Nicholas.
Frequently, his prose
was peppered with
amusing verse, like this
poem about the camel.

The Frog

Be kind and tender to the Frog
      And do not call him names,
As "Slimy-skin," or "Polly-wog,"
      Or likewise "Uncle James,"
Or "Gape-a-grin," or "Toad-gone-wrong,"
      Or "Billy Bandy-knees":
The frog is justly sensitive
      To epithets like these.

No animal will more repay
      A treatment kind and fair,
At least, so lonely people say
Who keep a frog (and by the way,
      They are extremely rare).

—HILAIRE BELLOC

Hilaire Belloc was an essayist, historian, novelist, and poet, but he is best known today for his light verse. His mother was English and his father French and he was educated in England. This poem about the frog is from his book *Bad Child's Book of Beasts.*

The Blind Men and the Elephant

It was six men of Indostan
    To learning much inclined,
Who went to see the elephant
    (Though all of them were blind),
That each by observation
    Might satisfy his mind.

The First approached the elephant,
    And, happening to fall
Against his broad and sturdy side,
    At once began to bawl:
"God bless me! but the elephant
    Is nothing but a wall!"

The Second, feeling of the tusk,
    Cried: "Ho! What have we here
So very round and smooth and sharp?
    To me 'tis mighty clear
This wonder of an elephant
    Is very like a spear!"

The Third approached the animal
    And, happening to take
The squirming trunk within his hands,
    Thus boldly up and spake:
"I see," quoth he, "the elephant
    Is very like a snake!"

The Fourth reached out his eager hand,
    And felt about the knee:

"What most this wondrous beast is like
      Is mighty plain," quoth he;
"'Tis clear enough the elephant
      Is very like a tree."

The Fifth, who chanced to touch the ear,
      Said: "E'en the blindest man
Can tell what this resembles most;
      Deny the fact who can,
This marvel of an elephant
      Is very like a fan!"

The Sixth no sooner had begun
      About the beast to grope,
Than, seizing on the swinging tail
      That fell within his scope,
"I see," quoth he, "the elephant
      Is very like a rope!"

And so these men of Indostan
      Disputed loud and long,
Each in his own opinion
      Exceeding stiff and strong,
Though each was partly in the right,
      And all were in the wrong!

So, oft in theologic wars
      The disputants, I ween,
Rail on in utter ignorance
      Of what each other mean,
And prate about an elephant
      Not one of them has seen!

—JOHN GODFREY SAXE

Born and educated in Vermont, John Godfrey Saxe was a lawyer and a journalist. He was editor of the Burlington, Vermont, *Sentinel*, served as the state's attorney general, and ran, unsuccessfully, for governor. His books of humorous verse were popular in their day, but now only this poem is remembered.

That Cat

The cat that comes to my window sill
When the moon looks cold and the night is still—
He comes in a frenzied state alone
With a tail that stands like a pine tree cone,
And says: "I have finished my evening lark,
And I think I can hear a hound dog bark.
My whiskers are froze 'nd stuck to my chin.
I do wish you'd git up and let me in."
      That cat gits in.

But if in the solitude of the night
He doesn't appear to be feeling right,
And rises and stretches and seeks the floor,
And some remote corner he would explore,
And doesn't feel satisfied just because
There's no good spot for to sharpen his claws,
And meows and canters uneasy about
Beyond the least shadow of any doubt
      That cat gits out.

—BEN KING

The Butterfly's Day

From cocoon forth a butterfly
As lady from her door
Emerged—a summer afternoon—
Repairing everywhere,

Without design, that I could trace,
Except to stray abroad
On miscellaneous enterprise
The clovers understood.

Her pretty parasol was seen
Contracting in a field
Where men made hay, then struggling hard
With an opposing cloud,

Where parties, phantom as herself,
To Nowhere seemed to go
In purposeless circumference,
As 't were a tropic show.

And notwithstanding bee that worked,
And flower that zealous blew,
This audience of idleness
Disdained them, from the sky,

Till sundown crept, a steady tide,
And men that made the hay,
And afternoon, and butterfly,
Extinguished in its sea.

–EMILY DICKINSON

The Hen

The hen is a ferocious fowl,
She pecks you till she makes you howl.

And all the time she flaps her wings,
And says the most insulting things.

And when you try to take her eggs,
She bites large pieces from your legs.

The only safe way to get these,
Is to creep on your hands and knees.

In the meanwhile a friend must hide,
And jump out on the other side.

And then you snatch the eggs and run,
While she pursues the other one.

The difficulty is, to find
A trusty friend who will not mind.

—LORD ALFRED DOUGLAS

The Eagle

He clasps the crag with crooked hands;
Close to the sun in lonely lands,
Ringed with the azure world, he stands.

The wrinkled sea beneath him crawls;
He watches from his mountain walls,
And like a thunderbolt he falls.

—ALFRED LORD TENNYSON

The Crocodile

How doth the little crocodile
    Improve his shining tail,
And pour the waters of the Nile
    On every golden scale!

How cheerfully he seems to grin,
    How neatly spreads his claws,
And welcomes little fishes in,
    With gently smiling jaws!

—LEWIS CARROLL

The Codfish

The codfish lays ten thousand eggs,
     The homely hen lays one.
The codfish never cackles
     To tell you what she's done.
And so we scorn the codfish,
     While the humble hen we prize,
Which only goes to show you
     That it pays to advertise.

—AUTHOR UNKNOWN

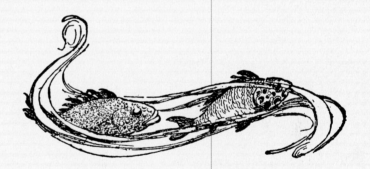

The Shark

A treacherous monster is the shark,
He never makes the least remark.

And when he sees you on the sand,
He doesn't seem to want to land.

He watches you take off your clothes,
And not the least excitement shows.

His eyes do not grow bright or roll,
He has astounding self-control.

He waits till you are quite undressed,
And seems to take no interest.

And when you once get in his range,
His whole demeanor seems to change.

He throws his body right about,
And his true character comes out.

It's no use crying or appealing,
He seems to lose all decent feeling.

After this warning you will wish
To keep clear of this treacherous fish.

His back is black, his stomach white,
He has a very dangerous bite.

–LORD ALFRED DOUGLAS

On the Grasshopper and the Cricket

The poetry of earth is never dead:
When all the birds are faint with the hot sun,
And hide in cooling trees, a voice will run
From hedge to hedge about the new-mown mead;
That is the Grasshopper's—he takes the lead
In summer luxury,—he has never done
With his delights; for when tired out with fun
He rests at ease beneath some pleasant weed.
The poetry of earth is ceasing never:
On a lone winter evening, when the frost
Has wrought a silence, from the stove there shrills
The Cricket's song, in warmth increasing ever,
And seems to one in drowsiness half lost,
The Grasshopper's among some grassy hills.

—JOHN KEATS

John Keats, an Englishman, wrote many great poems before his death at the age of twenty-five. His poems are exceptionally clear and simple and he had the ability to draw the reader into a world of beautiful sounds and images.

To a Butterfly

I've watched you now a full half hour
Self-poised upon that yellow flower;
And, little butterfly, indeed,
I know not if you sleep or feed.

How motionless!—not frozen seas
      More motionless; and then,
What joy awaits you when the breeze
Hath found you out among the trees,
      And calls you forth again!

This plot of orchard ground is ours,
My trees they are, my sister's flowers;
Here rest your wings when they are weary,
Here lodge as in a sanctuary!

Come to us often, fear no wrong,
      Sit near us on the bough!
We'll talk of sunshine and of song,
And summer days when we were young;
Sweet childish days that were as long
      As twenty days are now.

—WILLIAM WORDSWORTH

William Wordsworth is one of English literature's most important and original poets. He is particularly renowned for his nature poetry.

The Snake

A narrow fellow in the grass
Occasionally rides;
You may have met him—did you not,
His notice sudden is.

The grass divides as with a comb,
A spotted shaft is seen;
And then it closes at your feet
And opens further on.

He likes a boggy acre,
A floor too cool for corn.
Yet when a child, and barefoot,
I more than once, at morn,

Have passed, I thought, a whip-lash
Unbraiding in the sun,—
When, stooping to secure it,
It wrinkled, and was gone.

Several of nature's people
I know, and they know me;
I feel for them a transport
Of cordiality;

But I never met this fellow,
Attended or alone,
Without a tighter breathing,
And zero at the bone.

–EMILY DICKINSON

The Bee

Like trains of cars on tracks of plush
        I hear the level bee:
A jar across the flowers goes,
        Their velvet masonry.

Withstands until the sweet assault
        Their chivalry consumes,
While he, victorious, tilts away
        To vanquish other blooms.

His feet are shod with gauze,
        His helmet is of gold;
His breast, a single onyx
        With chrysoprase, inlaid.

His labor is a chant,
        His idleness a tune;
Oh, for a bee's experience
        Of clovers and of noon!

—EMILY DICKINSON

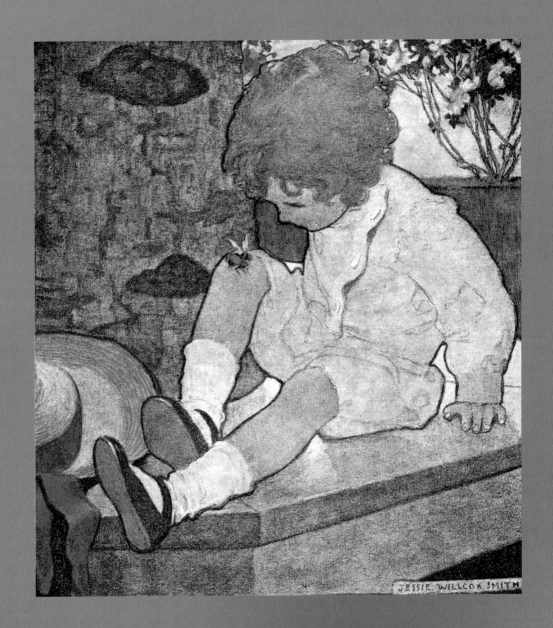

Two Birds and Their Nest

Two guests from Alabama—two together,
And their nest, and four light-green eggs,
    spotted with brown,
And every day the he-bird, to and fro, near at hand,
And every day the she-bird, crouch'd on her nest,
    silent, with bright eyes,
And every day I, a curious boy, never too close,
    never disturbing them,
Cautiously peering.

—WALT WHITMAN

Walt Whitman was born on Long Island, New York, in 1819, and grew up in Brooklyn. He worked as a printer, newspaperman, and schoolteacher. In 1855, he published the first edition of *Leaves of Grass*, a book of highly original poetry which he enlarged throughout his life.

The Chameleon

The chameleon changes his color;
      He can look like a tree or a wall;
He is timid and shy and he hates to be seen,
So he simply sits down on the grass and grows green,
      And pretends he is nothing at all.

I wish I could change my complexion
      To purple or orange or red:
I wish I could look like the arm of a chair
So nobody ever would know I was there
      When they wanted to put me to bed.

I wish I could be a chameleon
      And look like a lily or rose;
I'd lie on the apples and peaches and pears,
But not on Aunt Margaret's yellowy chairs—
      I should have to be careful of those.

The chameleon's life is confusing;
      He is used to adventure and pain;
But if he ever sat on Aunt Maggie's cretonne
And found what a curious color he'd gone,
      I don't think he'd do it again.

—A. P. HERBERT

Caterpillar

Brown and furry
Caterpillar in a hurry,
Take your walk
To the shady leaf, or stalk,
Or what not,
Which may be the chosen spot.
No toad spy you,
Hovering bird of prey pass by you;
Spin and die,
To live again a butterfly.

—CHRISTINA ROSSETTI

Christina Georgina Rossetti, who is among the great English poets, was born in London. Her father was Italian and her mother half Italian. She was educated at home and spoke Italian as fluently as English. From childhood, however, her health was bad and she spent much of her life as an invalid within the family circle. Although she was timid and cloistered, in her poetry her spirit soared to greatness.

The Snail

The frugal snail, with forecast of repose,
Carries his house with him wherever he goes,
Peeps out—and if there comes a shower of rain,
Retreats to his small domicile amain.
Touch but a tip of him, a horn—'tis well—
He curls up in his sanctuary shell.
He's his own landlord, his own tenant, stay
Long as he will, he dreads no Quarter Day.
Himself he boards, and lodges, both invites
And feasts himself; sleeps with himself o'nights.
He spares the upholsterer trouble to procure
Chattels, himself is his own furniture,
And his sole riches. Whereso'er he roam—
Knock when you will—he's sure to be at home.

—CHARLES LAMB

Charles Lamb was born in London in 1775 and lived there for his whole life. He held a number of government jobs, and wrote poetry and essays. He is best-known today for *Tales of Shakespeare*, the children's book which he wrote with his sister, Mary.

MEET THE FAMILY

Many poets have written about their families, the things they do together,

and the homes they live in. Some of the poems in this section are funny,

others are serious, but they are all about members of the family—

mothers, fathers, sisters and brothers, grandmothers and grandfathers,

sons and daughters, and even a cousin or two.

When Mother
Reads Aloud

When Mother reads aloud, the past
      Seems real as every day;
I hear the tramp of armies vast,
I see the spears and lances cast,
      I join the thrilling fray;
Brave knights and ladies fair and proud
I meet when Mother reads aloud.

When Mother reads aloud, far lands
      Seem very near and true;
I cross the desert's gleaming sands,
Or hunt the jungle's prowling bands,
      Or sail the ocean blue.
Far heights, whose peaks the cold mists shroud,
I scale, when Mother reads aloud.

When Mother reads aloud, I long
      For noble deeds to do—
To help the right, redress the wrong;
It seems so easy to be strong,
      So simple to be true.
Oh, thick and fast the visions crowd
My eyes, when Mother reads aloud.

—AUTHOR UNKNOWN

The Reading Mother

I had a mother who read to me
Sagas of pirates who scoured the sea,
Cutlasses clenched in their yellow teeth,
"Blackbirds" stowed in the hold beneath.

I had a mother who read me lays
Of ancient and gallant and golden days;
Stories of Marmion and Ivanhoe,
Which every boy has a right to know.

I had a mother who read me tales
Of Gelert the hound of the hills of Wales,
True to his trust till his tragic death,
Faithfulness blent with his final breath.

I had a mother who read me the things
That wholesome life to the boy heart brings—
Stories that stir with an upward touch,
Oh, that each mother of boys were such!

You may have tangible wealth untold;
Caskets of jewels and coffers of gold,
Richer than I you can never be—
I had a mother who read to me.

—STRICKLAND W. GILLILAN

The Children's Hour

Between the dark and the daylight,
    When the night is beginning to lower,
Comes a pause in the day's occupations
    That is known as the children's hour.

I hear in the chamber above me
    The patter of little feet,
The sound of a door that is opened,
    And voices soft and sweet.

From my study I see in the lamplight,
    Descending the broad hall stair,
Grave Alice, and laughing Allegra,
    And Edith with golden hair.

A whisper, and then a silence:
    Yet I know by their merry eyes
They are plotting and planning together
    To take me by surprise.

A sudden rush from the stairway,
    A sudden raid from the hall!
By three doors left unguarded
    They enter my castle wall!

They climb up into my turret
    O'er the arms and back of my chair;
If I try to escape, they surround me;
    They seem to be everywhere.

They almost devour me with kisses,
      Their arms about me entwine,
Till I think of the Bishop of Bingen
      In his Mouse Tower on the Rhine!

Do you think, O blue-eyed banditti,
      Because you have scaled the wall,
Such an old mustache as I am
      Is not a match for you all?

I have you fast in my fortress,
      And will not let you depart,
But put you down into the dungeon
      In the round tower of my heart.

And there I will keep you forever,
      Yes, forever and a day,
Till the wall shall crumble to ruin,
      And molder in dust away!

—HENRY WADSWORTH LONGFELLOW

Henry Wadsworth Longfellow is one of the most popular poets who ever lived. Born in Portland, Maine, he taught modern languages at Harvard. He wrote this poem for his daughter Edith, whose golden hair is mentioned.

A Boy and His Dad

A boy and his dad on a fishing trip—
There is a glorious fellowship!
Father and son and the open sky
And the white clouds lazily drifting by,
And the laughing stream as it runs along
With the clicking reel like a martial song,
And the father teaching the youngster gay
How to land a fish in the sportsman's way.

Which is happier, man or boy?
The soul of the father is steeped in joy,
For he's finding out, to his heart's delight,
That his son is fit for the future fight.
He is learning the glorious depths of him,
And the thoughts he thinks and his every whim,
And he shall discover, when night comes on,
How close he has grown to his little son.

A boy and his dad on a fishing trip—
Oh, I envy them, as I see them there
Under the sky in the open air,
For out of the old, old long ago
Come the summer days that I used to know,
When I learned life's truths from my father's lips
As I shared the joy of his fishing trips—
Builders of life's companionship!

—EDGAR A. GUEST

Edgar A. Guest, who was born in Birmingham, England, was brought to the United States as a boy. When he was twenty, he began writing a daily poem for the *Detroit Free Press*. For more than fifty years these poems were syndicated to newspapers all over the country. His widely read poems were much admired for their happy quality.

Mother's Jewels

Aunt Eleanor wears such diamonds!
　　Shiny and gay and grand,
Some on her neck and some in her hair,
　　And some on her pretty hand.
One day I asked my mama
　　Why she never wore them, too;
She laughed and said, as she kissed my eyes,
　　"My jewels are here, bright blue.
They laugh and dance and beam and smile,
　　So lovely all the day,
And never like Aunt Eleanor's go
　　In a velvet box to stay.
Hers are prisoned in bands of gold,
　　But mine are free as air,
Set in a bonny, dimpled face,
　　And shadowed with shining hair!"

–EUGENE FIELD

Eugene Field, an American, worked for a number of newspapers before he became a columnist for the *Chicago Morning News.* He was very fond of children and wrote many poems for and about them. There is a statue of Eugene Field in Lincoln Park in Chicago.

Choosing a Name

I have got a new born sister;
I was nigh the first that kissed her.
When the nursing-woman brought her
To Papa, his infant daughter,
How Papa's dear eyes did glisten!
She will shortly be to christen;

And Papa has made the offer,
I shall have the naming of her.

Now I wonder what would please her,
Charlotte, Julia, or Louisa?
Ann and Mary, they're too common;
Joan's too formal for a woman;
Jane's a prettier name beside;
But we had a Jane that died.
They would say, if 't was Rebecca,
That she was a little Quaker.
Edith's pretty, but that looks
Better in Old English books;
Ellen's left off long ago;
Blanche is out of fashion now.
None that I have named as yet
Are so good as Margaret.
Emily is neat and fine;
What do you think of Caroline?
How I'm puzzled and perplexed
What to choose or think of next!
I am in a little fever
Lest the name that I should give her
Should disgrace her or defame her;
I shall leave Papa to name her.

—MARY LAMB

My Little Girl

My little girl is nested
  Within her tiny bed,
With amber ringlets crested
  Around her dainty head;
She lies so calm and stilly,
  She breathes so soft and low,
She calls to mind a lily
  Half-hidden in the snow.

A weary little mortal
  Has gone to slumberland;
The pixies at the portal
  Have caught her by the hand.
She dreams her broken dolly
  Will soon be mended there,
That looks so melancholy
  Upon the rocking chair.

I kiss your wayward tresses,
  My drowsy little queen;
I know you have caresses
  From floating forms unseen.
O, angels, let me keep her
  To kiss away my cares,
This darling little sleeper,
  Who has my love and prayers!

—SAMUEL MINTURN PECK

Brother and Sister

I cannot choose but think upon the time
When our two lives grew like two buds that kiss
At lightest thrill from the bee's swinging chime,
Because the one so near the other is.
He was the elder and a little man
Of forty inches, bound to show no dread,
And I the girl that puppy-like now ran,
Now lagged behind my brother's larger tread.
I held him wise, and when he talked to me
Of snakes and birds, and which God loved the best,
I thought his knowledge marked the boundary
Where men grew blind, though angels knew the rest.
      If he said "Hush!" I tried to hold my breath;
      Wherever he said "Come!" I stepped in faith.

Those long days measured by my little feet
Had chronicles which yield me many a text;
Where irony still finds an image meet
Of full-grown judgments in this world perplext.
One day my brother left me in high charge,
To mind the rod, while he went seeking bait,
And bade me, when I saw a nearing barge,
Snatch out the line, lest he should come too late.
Proud of the task, I watched with all my might
For one whole minute, till my eyes grew wide,
Till sky and earth took on a strange new light
And seemed a dream-world floating on some tide—
      A fair pavilioned boat for me alone
      Bearing me onward through the vast unknown.

These four sonnets are from "Brother and Sister," a sequence of eleven poems, in which the novelist George Eliot (the pseudonym of Mary Ann Evans) tells of her childhood relationship with her brother, Isaac Evans. She explored this relationship further in her novel *The Mill on the Floss.*

But sudden came the barge's pitch-black prow,
Nearer and angrier came my brother's cry,
And all my soul was quivering fear, when lo!
Upon the imperiled line, suspended high,
A silver perch! My guilt that won the prey,
Now turned to merit, had a guerdon rich
Of hugs and praises, and made merry play,
Until my triumph reached its highest pitch
When all at home were told the wondrous feat,
And how the little sister had fished well.
In secret, though my fortune tasted sweet,
I wondered why this happiness befell.
      "The little lass had luck," the gardener said:
      And so I learned, luck was with glory wed.

School parted us; we never found again
That childish world where our two spirits mingled
Like scents from varying roses that remain
One sweetness, nor can evermore be singled.
Yet the twin habit of that early time
Lingered for long about the heart and tongue:
We had been natives of one happy clime,
And its dear accent to our utterance clung,
Till the dire years whose awful name is Change
Had grasped our souls still yearning in divorce,
And pitiless shaped them in two forms that range
Two elements which sever their life's course.
      But were another childhood-world my share,
      I would be born a little sister there.

—GEORGE ELIOT

Our Son

He's supposed to be our son, our hope and our pride,
In him all the dreams of our future abide,
But whenever some act to his credit occurs
I never am mentioned, the glory is hers,
And whenever he's bad or has strayed from the line,
Then always she speaks of the rascal as mine.

When trouble has come she will soberly say:
"Do you know what your son has been up to today?
Your son spilled the ink on the living-room floor!
Your son broke the glass in the dining-room door!
I am telling you now something has to be done,
It is high time you started correcting your son!"

But when to the neighbors she boasts of his worth,
It is: "My son's the best little boy on the earth!"
Accuse him of mischief, she'll just floor you flat
With: "My son, I'm certain, would never do that!
Of course there are times when he's willfully bad
But then it's that temper he gets from his dad!"

—EDGAR A. GUEST

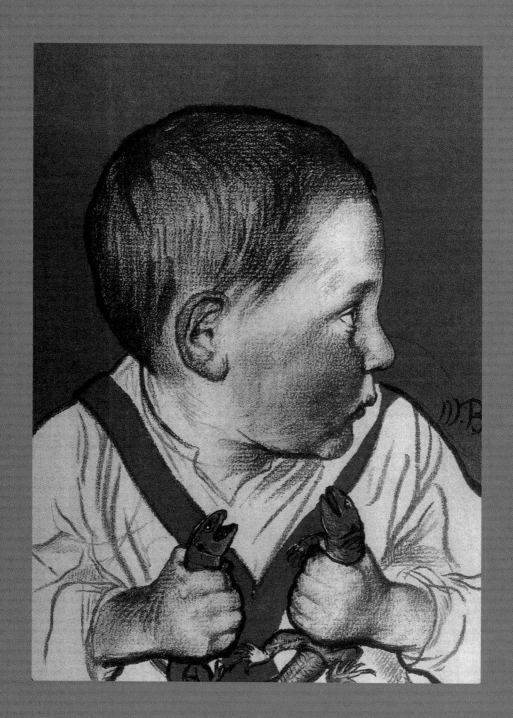

The New England Boy's Song About Thanksgiving Day

Over the river, and through the wood,
    To Grandfather's house we go;
        The horse knows the way,
        To carry the sleigh,
    Through the white and drifted snow.

Over the river, and through the wood,
    To Grandfather's house away!
        We would not stop
        For doll or top,
    For 'tis Thanksgiving day.

Over the river, and through the wood,
    With a clear blue winter sky,
        The dogs do bark,
        And children hark,
    As we go jingling by.

Over the river, and through the wood,
    To have a first-rate play—
        Hear the bells ring
        Ting a ling ding,
    Hurrah for Thanksgiving day!

Over the river, and through the wood—
    No matter for winds that blow;

Lydia Maria Child was born in Medford, Massachusetts, the daughter of a baker. When she was twenty-two years old she published a novel called *Hobomok*. Two years later she began *The Juvenile Miscellany*, the first American magazine for children. This poem about Thanksgiving Day in New England is often sung.

Or if we get
The sleigh upset,
Into a bank of snow.

Over the river, and through the wood,
To see little John and Ann;
We will kiss them all,
And play snowball,
And stay as long as we can.

Over the river, and through the wood,
Trot fast, my dapple gray!
Spring over the ground,
Like a hunting hound,
For 'tis Thanksgiving day!

Over the river, and through the wood,
And straight through the barnyard gate;
We seem to go
Extremely slow,
It is so hard to wait.

Over the river, and through the wood—
Old Jowler hears our bells;
He shakes his paw
With a loud bow wow,
And thus the news he tells.

Over the river, and through the wood—
When Grandmother sees us come,
She will say, Oh dear,
The children are here,
Bring a pie for every one.

Over the river, and through the wood—
    Now Grandmother's cap I spy!
        Hurrah for the fun!
        Is the pudding done?
    Hurrah for the pumpkin pie!

–LYDIA MARIA CHILD

To a New Baby

Little kicking, cuddling thing,
You don't cry—you only sing!
Blinking eyes and stubby nose,
Mouth that mocks the budding rose,
Down for hair, peach-blows for hands—
Ah–h–h–h! Of all the "baby-grands"
Any one could wish to see,
You're the finest one for me!

Skin as soft as velvet is:
God (when you were only his)
Touched you on the cheek and chin—
Where he touched are dimples in.
Creases on your wrists, as though
Strings were fastened 'round them so
We could tie you tight and keep
You from leaving while we sleep.

Once I tried to look at you
From a stranger's point of view;
You were red and wrinkled; then
I just loved, and looked again;
What I saw was not the same;
In my eyes the blessed flame
Of a father's love consumed
Faults to strangers' eyes illumed.

Little squirming, cuddling thing!
Ere you shed each angel wing,
Did they tell you you were sent
With a cargo of content
To a home down here below
Where they hungered for you so?
Do you know, you flawless pearl,
How we love our baby girl?

−STRICKLAND W. GILLILAN

"One, Two, Three"

It was an old, old, old, old lady,
    And a boy who was half-past three;
And the way that they played together
    Was beautiful to see.

She couldn't go romping and jumping,
    And the boy no more could he;
For he was a thin little fellow,
    With a thin little twisted knee.

They sat in the yellow sunlight,
    Out under the maple tree;
And the game they played I'll tell you,
    Just as it was told to me.

It was Hide-and-Go-Seek they were playing,
    Though you'd never have known it to be—
With an old, old, old, old lady,
    And a boy with a twisted knee.

The boy would bend his face down
    On his little sound right knee,
And he'd guess where she was hiding
    In guesses One, Two, Three.

"You are in the china closet!"
    He would laugh and cry with glee—
It wasn't the china closet,
    But he still had Two and Three.

"You are up in Papa's big bedroom,
        In the chest with the queer old key!"
And she said, "You are warm and warmer;
        But you are not quite right," said she.

"It can't be the little cupboard
        Where Mamma's things used to be—
So it must be in the little clothes press, Gran'ma,"
        And he found her with his Three.

Then she covered her face with her fingers,
        That were wrinkled and white and wee,
And she guessed where the boy was hiding,
        With a One and a Two and a Three.

And they never had stirred from their places
        Right under the maple tree—
This old, old, old, old lady
        And the boy with the lame little knee—
This dear, dear, dear, dear old lady,
        And the boy who was half-past three.

–HENRY CUYLER BUNNER

JUST ME

Many poems are autobiographical. Poets often write about themselves.

They write about their experiences and their dreams, as

well as what they feel—happiness, excitement, even sadness.

All the poems in this section fit into this category.

Afternoon on a Hill

I will be the gladdest thing
    Under the sun!
I will touch a hundred flowers
    And not pick one.

I will look at cliffs and clouds
    With quiet eyes,
Watch the wind bow down the grass,
    And the grass rise.

And when lights begin to show
    Up from the town,
I will mark where must be mine,
    And then start down!

—EDNA ST. VINCENT MILLAY

Edna St. Vincent Millay was born in Maine and was a graduate of Vassar. When she was only nineteen years old her poem "Renascence" was published and not long after that she became the country's most admired woman poet.

My Shadow

I have a little shadow that goes in and out with me,
And what can be the use of him is more than I can see.
He is very, very like me from the heels up to the head,
And I see him jump before me, when I jump into my bed.

The funniest thing about him is the way he likes to grow—
Not at all like proper children, which is always very slow;
For he sometimes shoots up taller, like an India-rubber ball,
And he sometimes gets so little that there's none of him at all.

–ROBERT LOUIS STEVENSON

Escape at Bedtime

The lights from the parlor and kitchen shone out
    Through the blinds and the windows and bars;
And high overhead and all moving about,
    There were thousands of millions of stars.
There ne'er were such thousands of leaves on a tree,
    Nor of people in church or the park,
As the crowds of the stars that looked down upon me,
    And that glittered and winked in the dark.

The Dog, and the Plough, and the Hunter, and all,
    And the star of the sailor, and Mars,
These shone in the sky, and the pail by the wall
    Would be half full of water and stars.
They saw me at last, and they chased me with cries,
    And they soon had me packed into bed;
But the glory kept shining and bright in my eyes,
    And the stars going round in my head.

—ROBERT LOUIS STEVENSON

Block City

What are you able to build with your blocks?
Castles and palaces, temples and docks.
Rain may keep raining, and others go roam,
But I can be happy and building at home,

Let the sofa be mountains, the carpet be sea,
There I'll establish a city for me:
A church and a mill and a palace beside,
And a harbor as well where my vessels may ride.

Great is the palace with pillar and wall,
A sort of a tower on the top of it all,
And steps coming down in an orderly way
To where my toy vessels lie safe in the bay.

This one is sailing and that one is moored:
Hark to the song of the sailors on board!
And see, on the steps of my palace, the kings
Coming and going with presents and things!

Now I have done with it, down let it go!
All in a moment the town is laid low.
Block upon block lying scattered and free,
What is there left of my town by the sea?

Yet as I saw it, I see it again,
The church and the palace, the ships and the men,
And as long as I live and where'er I may be,
I'll always remember my town by the sea.

–ROBERT LOUIS STEVENSON

Seven Times One

There's no dew left on the daisies and clover,
    There's no rain left in heaven:
I've said my "seven times" over and over,
    Seven times one are seven.

I am old, so old, I can write a letter;
    My birthday lessons are done;
The lambs play always, they know no better;
    They are only one times one.

O moon! in the night I have seen you sailing
    And shining so round and low;
You were bright! ah, bright! but your light is failing—
    You are nothing now but a bow.

You moon, have you done something wrong in heaven
    That God has hidden your face?
I hope if you have you will soon be forgiven,
    And shine again in your place.

O velvet bee, you're a dusty fellow,
    You've powdered your legs with gold!
O brave marsh maybuds, rich and yellow,
    Give me your money to hold!

O columbine, open your folded wrapper,
    Where two twin turtledoves dwell!
O cuckoopint, toll me the purple clapper
    That hangs in your clear, green bell!

And show me your nest with the young ones in it,
    I will not steal them away;
I am old! you may trust me, linnet, linnet—
    I am seven times one today.

—JEAN INGELOW

Me

As long as I live
I shall always be
My Self—and no other,
Just me.

Like a tree.

Like a willow or elder,
An aspen, a thorn,
Or a cypress forlorn.

Like a flower,
For its hour
A primrose, a pink,
Or a violet—
Sunned by the sun,
And with dewdrops wet.

Always just me.

—WALTER DE LA MARE

Walter de la Mare, a gifted writer, was born in England in 1873. His family was poor and at the age of eighteen he went to work as a bookkeeper and it was not until he was thirty-six that he was able to move to the country and devote all his time to his writing. He published more than fifty volumes of poetry, short stories, essays, and novels. He is best known for his truly imaginative verse for children.

The Land of Counterpane

When I was sick and lay a-bed
I had two pillows at my head,
And all my toys beside me lay
To keep me happy all the day.

And sometimes for an hour or so
I watched my leaden soldiers go,
With different uniforms and drills,
Among the bedclothes, through the hills;

And sometimes sent my ships in fleets
All up and down among the sheets;
Or brought my trees and houses out,
And planted cities all about.

I was the giant great and still
That sits upon the pillow-hill,
And sees before him, dale and plain,
The pleasant land of counterpane.

–ROBERT LOUIS STEVENSON

In the Summer When I Go to Bed

In the summer when I go to bed
The sun still streaming overhead
My bed becomes so small and hot
With sheets and pillow in a knot,
And then I lie and try to see
The things I'd really like to be.

I think I'd be a glossy cat
A little plump, but not too fat.
I'd never touch a bird or mouse
I'm much too busy round the house.

And then a fierce and hungry hound
The king of dogs for miles around;
I'd chase the postman just for fun
To see how quickly he could run.

Perhaps I'd be a crocodile
Within the marshes of the Nile
And paddle in the riverbed
With dripping mud caps on my head.

Or maybe next a mountain goat
With shaggy whiskers at my throat,
Leaping streams and jumping rocks
In stripey pink and purple socks.

Or else I'd be a polar bear
And on an iceberg make my lair;

Thomas Hood, who wrote this poem, was an Englishman who lived more than one hundred years ago. His father, who was also a writer, had the same name and so he was known as Thomas, the younger, or Tom. He wrote novels for adults and also wrote and illustrated many books for children.

I'd keep a shop in Baffin Sound
To sell icebergs by the pound.

And then I'd be a wise old frog
Squatting on a sunken log,
I'd teach the fishes lots of games
And how to read and write their names.

An Indian lion then I'd be
And lounge about on my settee;
I'd feed on nothing but bananas
And spend all day in my pajamas.

I'd like to be a tall giraffe
Making lots of people laugh,
I'd do a tap dance in the street
With little bells upon my feet.

And then I'd be a fozy fox
Streaking through the hollyhocks,
Horse or hound would ne'er catch me
I'm a master of disguise, you see.

I think I'd be a chimpanzee
With musical ability,
I'd play a silver clarinet
Or form a Monkey String Quartet.

And then a snake with scales of gold
Guarding hoards of wealth untold,
No thief would dare to steal a pin—
But friends of mine I would let in.

But then before I really know
Just what I'd be or where I'd go
My bed becomes so wide and deep
And all my thoughts are fast asleep.

–THOMAS HOOD

Life Doesn't Frighten Me

Shadows on the wall
Noises down the hall
Life doesn't frighten me at all
Bad dogs barking loud
Big ghosts in a cloud
Life doesn't frighten me at all.

Mean old Mother Goose
Lions on the loose
They don't frighten me at all
Dragons breathing flame
On my counterpane
That doesn't frighten me at all.

I go boo
Make them shoo
I make fun
Way they run
I won't cry

So they fly
I just smile
They go wild
Life doesn't frighten me at all.

Tough guys in a fight
All alone at night
Life doesn't frighten me at all.
Panthers in the park
Strangers in the dark
No, they don't frighten me at all.

That new classroom where
Boys all pull my hair
(Kissy little girls
With their hair in curls)
They don't frighten me at all.

Don't show me frogs and snakes
And listen for my scream,
If I'm afraid at all
It's only in my dreams.

I've got a magic charm
That I keep up my sleeve,
I can walk the ocean floor
And never have to breathe.

Life doesn't frighten me at all
Not at all
Not at all.
Life doesn't frighten me at all.

—MAYA ANGELOU

Maya Angelou, who
wrote and recited a
poem for President Bill
Clinton's inauguration,
has written five
collections of poetry; has
worked in the theater
as a director, actor, and
writer; was active in the
Civil Rights movement;
and has received many
honorary degrees.

Just Me

Nobody sees what I can see,
For back of my eyes there is only me.
And nobody knows how my thoughts begin,
For there's only myself inside my skin.
Isn't it strange how everyone owns
Just enough skin to cover his bones?
My father's would be too big to fit—
I'd be all wrinkled inside of it.
And my baby brother's is much too small—
It just wouldn't cover me up at all.
But I feel just right in the skin I wear,
And there's nobody like me anywhere.

—MARGARET HILLERT

FRIENDSHIP AND LOVE

One of the best gifts to give or receive

is the gift of friendship. Most of the poems in this section

celebrate what it means to be a friend. Some of them also

speak about how wonderful it is to be loved.

Love and Friendship

Love is like the wild rose briar,
Friendship is like the holly tree—
The holly is dark when the rose briar blooms
But which will bloom more constantly?

The wild rose briar is sweet in spring,
Its summer blossoms scent the air;
Yet wait till winter comes again
And who will call the wild briar fair?

Then scorn the silly rose wreath now
And deck thee with the holly's sheen,
That when December blights thy brow
He still may leave thy garland green.

—EMILY BRONTË

Emily Brontë, the sister of Charlotte Brontë, is best known as the author of the novel *Wuthering Heights*, but she was also a fine poet.

A Boy's Song

Where the pools are bright and deep,
Where the gray trout lies asleep,
Up the river and o'er the lea—
That's the way for Billy and me.

Where the blackbird sings the latest,
Where the hawthorn blooms the sweetest,
Where the nestlings chirp and flee—
That's the way for Billy and me.

Where the mowers mow the cleanest,
Where the hay lies thick and greenest,
There to trace the homeward bee—
That's the way for Billy and me.

Where the hazel bank is steepest,
Where the shadow lies the deepest,
Where the clustering nuts fall free—
That's the way for Billy and me.

Why the boys should drive away
Little maidens from their play,
Or love to banter and fight so well,
That's the thing I never could tell.

But this I know: I love to play,
Through the meadow, among the hay.
Up the water and o'er the lea,
That's the way for Billy and me.

–JAMES HOGG

Laughing Song

When the green woods laugh with the voice of joy,
And the dimpling stream runs laughing by;
When the air does laugh with our merry wit,
And the green hill laughs with the noise of it;

When the meadows laugh with lively green,
And the grasshopper laughs in the merry scene;
When Mary and Susan and Emily
With their sweet round mouths sing "Ha, Ha, He!"

When the painted birds laugh in the shade,
When our table with cherries and nuts is spread:
Come live, and be merry, and join with me,
To sing the sweet chorus of "Ha, Ha, He!"

—WILLIAM BLAKE

Rondeau

Jenny kissed me when we met,
      Jumping from the chair she sat in;
Time, you thief, who loves to get
      Sweets into your list, put that in:
Say I'm weary, say I'm sad,
      Say that health and wealth have missed me,
Say I'm growing old, but add,
      Jenny kissed me.

—LEIGH HUNT

Leigh Hunt was a London journalist, essayist, and poet who crusaded for the abolition of slavery and child labor and was jailed for two years. This rondeau is one of his most popular poems. He wrote it for Jenny Carlyle, the wife of his friend Thomas, who was so delighted to see him after he had been ill for some weeks that she jumped up and kissed him.

The Pasture

I'm going out to clean the pasture spring;
I'll only stop to rake the leaves away
(And wait to watch the water clear, I may):
I sha'nt be gone long.—You come too.

I'm going out to fetch the little calf
That's standing by the mother. It's so young,
It totters when she licks it with her tongue.
I sha'nt be gone long.—You come too.

—ROBERT FROST

Robert Frost was born in San Francisco, but he moved to New England when he was ten years old and thus became the New England poet of the twentieth century.

LAUGHING LYRICS

This section is devoted to poems that are guaranteed to make you laugh, and laugh, and laugh. Some of them are nonsense verse—funny because they don't really make any sense. Others were written about funny people, or unlikely situations, or impossible events. Hillaire Belloc, Edward Lear, and Lewis Carroll are among the masters of light verse whose poems are included.

The Mock Turtle's Song

"Will you walk a little faster?" said a whiting to a snail,
"There's a porpoise close behind us, and he's treading on
    my tail.
See how eagerly the lobsters and the turtles all advance?
They are waiting on the shingle—will you come and join
    the dance?
Will you, won't you, will you, won't you, will you join
    the dance?
Will you, won't you, will you, won't you, won't you join
    the dance?

"You can really have no notion how delightful it will be,
When they take us up and throw us, with the lobsters,
    out to sea!"
But the snail replied, "Too far, too far!" and gave a look
    askance—
Said he thanked the whiting kindly, but he would not join
    the dance.
Would not, could not, would not, could not, would not join
    the dance.
Would not, could not, would not, could not, could not join
    the dance.

"What matters it how far we go?" his scaly friend replied,
"There is another shore, you know, upon the other side.
The further off from England the nearer is to France—
Then turn not pale, beloved snail, but come and join
    the dance.

This poem is from *Alice's Adventures in Wonderland*, which Lewis Carroll was inspired to write on a boat trip he made with Alice Liddell, the young daughter of the dean of the college where he taught mathematics, and her two sisters, Lorina and Edith.

Will you, won't you, will you, won't you, will you join
      the dance?
Will you, won't you, will you, won't you, won't you join
      the dance?"

–LEWIS CARROLL

The Yak

As a friend to the children commend me the Yak
You will find it exactly the thing:
It will carry and fetch, you can ride on its back,
      Or lead it about with a string.

The Tartar who dwells on the plains of Tibet
      (A desolate region of snow)
Has for centuries made it a nursery pet,
      And surely the Tartar should know!

Then tell your daddy where the Yak can be got,
      And if he is awfully rich
He will buy you the creature—or else he will not.
      (I cannot be positive which.)

–HILAIRE BELLOC

A Tragic Story

There lived a sage in days of yore,
And he a handsome pigtail wore:
But wondered much, and sorrowed more,
    Because it hung behind him.

He mused upon this curious case,
And swore he'd change the pigtail's place,
And have it hanging at his face,
    Not dangling there behind him.

Says he, "The mystery I've found—
I'll turn me round,"—
He turned him round;
    But still it hung behind him.

Then round, and round, and out and in,
All day the puzzled sage did spin;
In vain—it mattered not a pin—
    The pigtail hung behind him.

And right and left, and round about,
And up and down, and in and out,
He turned; but still the pigtail stout
    Hung steadily behind him.

And though his efforts never slack,
And though he twist, and twirl, and tack,
Alas! still faithful to his back,
    The pigtail hangs behind him.

—WILLIAM MAKEPEACE THACKERAY

A Trip to Morrow

I started on a journey just about a week ago
For the little town of Morrow in the State of Ohio.
I never was a traveler and really didn't know
That Morrow had been ridiculed a century or so.
I went down to the depot for my ticket and applied
For tips regarding Morrow, interviewed the station guide.
Said I, "My friend, I want to go to Morrow and return
Not later than tomorrow, for I haven't time to burn."

Said he to me, "Now let me see, if I have heard you right,
You want to go to Morrow and come back tomorrow night.
You should have gone to Morrow yesterday and back today,
For if you started yesterday to Morrow, don't you see
You should have got to Morrow and returned today at three.
The train that started yesterday, now understand me right,
Today it gets to Morrow and returns tomorrow night."

"Now if you start to Morrow, you will surely land
Tomorrow into Morrow, not today you understand,
For the train today to Morrow, if the schedule is right
Will get you into Morrow by about tomorrow night."
Said I, "I guess you know it all, but kindly let me say,
How can I go to Morrow if I leave the town today?"
Said he, "You cannot go to Morrow any more today,
For the train that goes to Morrow is a mile upon its way."

–AUTHOR UNKNOWN

The Walrus and the Carpenter

The sun was shining on the sea,
        Shining with all his might:
He did his very best to make
        The billows smooth and bright—
And this was odd, because it was
        The middle of the night.

The moon was shining sulkily,
        Because she thought the sun
Had got no business to be there
        After the day was done—
"It's very rude of him," she said,
        "To come and spoil the fun!"

The sea was wet as wet could be,
        The sands were dry as dry.
You could not see a cloud, because
        No cloud was in the sky:
No birds were flying overhead—
        There were no birds to fly.

The Walrus and the Carpenter
        Were walking close at hand:
They wept like anything to see
        Such quantities of sand:
"If this were only cleared away,"
        They said, "it would be grand!"

Lewis Carroll, who was an ordained minister, an accomplished mathematician and classicist, and an excellent photographer, stammered and was extremely shy. His real name was Charles Lutwidge Dodgson. To create his pseudonym, he dropped his last name, reversed the order of his first and middle names and then converted them to names deriving from Latin.

"If seven maids with seven mops
        Swept it for half a year,
Do you suppose," the Walrus said,
        "That they could get it clear?"
"I doubt it," said the Carpenter,
        And shed a bitter tear.

"O Oysters, come and walk with us!"
        The Walrus did beseech
"A pleasant walk, a pleasant talk,
        Along the briny beach:
We cannot do with more than four,
        To give a hand to each."

The eldest Oyster looked at him,
        But never a word he said:
The eldest Oyster winked his eye,
        And shook his heavy head—
Meaning to say he did not choose
        To leave the oyster bed.

But four young Oysters hurried up,
        All eager for the treat:
Their coats were brushed, their faces washed,
        Their shoes were clean and neat—
And this was odd, because, you know,
        They hadn't any feet.

Four other Oysters followed them,
        And yet another four;
And thick and fast they came at last,
        And more, and more, and more—

All hopping through the frothy waves,
  And scrambling to the shore.

The Walrus and the Carpenter
  Walked on a mile or so,
And then they rested on a rock
  Conveniently low.
And all the little Oysters stood
  And waited in a row.

"The time has come," the Walrus said,
  "To talk of many things,
Of shoes—and ships—and sealing wax—
  Of cabbages—and kings—
And why the sea is boiling hot—
  And whether pigs have wings."

"But wait a bit," the Oysters cried,
  "Before we have our chat;
For some of us are out of breath,
  And all of us are fat!"
"No hurry!" said the Carpenter.
  They thanked him much for that.

"A loaf of bread," the Walrus said,
  "Is what we chiefly need:
Pepper and vinegar besides
  Are very good indeed—
Now, if you're ready, Oysters dear,
  We can begin to feed."

"But not on us!" the Oysters cried,
  Turning a little blue.

"After such kindness, that would be
      A dismal thing to do!"
"The night is fine," the Walrus said.
      "Do you admire the view?

"It was so kind of you to come!
      And you are very nice!"
The Carpenter said nothing but
      "Cut us another slice.
I wish you were not quite so deaf—
      I've had to ask you twice!"

"It seems a shame," the Walrus said,
      "To play them such a trick.
After we've brought them out so far,
      And made them trot so quick!"
The Carpenter said nothing but
      "The butter's spread too thick!"

"I weep for you," the Walrus said:
      "I deeply sympathize,"
With sobs and tears he sorted out
      Those of the largest size,
Holding his pocket handkerchief
      Before his streaming eyes.

"O Oysters," said the Carpenter,
      "You've had a pleasant run!
Shall we be trotting home again!"
      But answer came there none—
And this was scarcely odd, because
      They'd eaten every one.

–LEWIS CARROLL

The Elf and the Dormouse

Under a toadstool crept a wee elf,
Out of the rain, to shelter himself.

Under the toadstool sound asleep,
Sat a big dormouse all in a heap.

Trembled the wee elf, frightened, and yet
Fearing to fly away lest he get wet.

To the next shelter—maybe a mile!
Sudden the wee elf smiled a wee smile.

Tugged till the toadstool toppled in two.
Holding it over him, gaily he flew.

Soon he was safe home, dry as could be.
Soon woke the dormouse—"Good gracious me!"

"Where is my toadstool?" loud he lamented,
And that's how umbrellas first were invented.

—OLIVER HERFORD

Oliver Herford was born in England but came to the United States when he was nineteen years old. He was an illustrator as well as a writer of poems and stories for adults and for children.

Have You Ever Seen?

Have you ever seen a sheet on a river bed?
Or a single hair from a hammer's head?
Has the foot of a mountain any toes?
And is there a pair of garden hose?

Does the needle ever wink its eye?
Why doesn't the wing of a building fly?
Can you tickle the ribs of a parasol?
Or open the trunk of a tree at all?

Are the teeth of a rake ever going to bite?
Have the hands of a clock any left or right?
Can the garden plot be deep and dark?
And what is the sound of the birch's bark?

–AUTHOR UNKNOWN

Words

Now, speech is very curious:
You never know what minute
A word will show a brand-new side,
With brand-new meaning in it.
This world could hardly turn around,
If some things acted like they sound.

Suppose the April flower beds,
Down in the garden spaces,
Were made with green frog-blanket spreads
And caterpillar cases;
Or oak trees locked their trunks to hide
The countless rings they keep inside!

Suppose from every pitcher plant
The milkweed came a-pouring;
That tiger lilies could be heard

With dandelions roaring,
Till all the cattails, far and near,
Began to bristle up in fear!

What if the old cow blew her horn
Some peaceful evening hour,
And suddenly a blast replied
From every trumpet flower,
While people's ears beat noisy drums
To "Hail the Conquering Hero Comes!"

If barnyard fowls had honeycombs,
What should we think, I wonder?
If lightning bugs should swiftly strike,
Then peal with awful thunder?
And would it turn our pink cheeks pale
To see a comet switch its tail?

—NANCY BYRD TURNER

The Purple Cow

I never saw a Purple Cow,
    I never hope to see one;
But I can tell you, anyhow,
    I'd rather see than be one.

—GELETT BURGESS

Gelett Burgess was born in Massachusetts, but for most of his life he lived in San Francisco. He wrote a lot of humorous fiction and poetry. This is his most famous nonsense poem. He also invented many words, like "goop" and "blurb," which are now part of the English language.

The Owl and the Pussy-Cat

The Owl and the Pussy-Cat went to sea
    In a beautiful pea-green boat,
They took some honey, and plenty of money,
    Wrapped up in a five-pound note.

The Owl looked up to the stars above,
    And sang to a small guitar,
"O lovely Pussy! O Pussy, my love,
    What a beautiful Pussy you are, you are!
    What a beautiful Pussy you are!"

Pussy said to the Owl, "You elegant fowl!
    How charmingly sweet you sing!
O let us be married! Too long we have tarried.
    But what shall we do for a ring?"

They sailed away for a year and a day,
    To the land where the Bong tree grows,
And there in a wood a Piggy-wig stood,
    With a ring at the end of his nose, his nose,
    With a ring at the end of his nose.

"Dear Pig, are you willing to sell for one shilling
    Your ring?" Said the Piggy, "I will."

So they took it away, and were married next day
    By the Turkey who lives on the hill.

Edward Lear traveled extensively—even to Egypt and India—as a watercolor painter of landscapes and birds. Among these were marvelous paintings of parrots. This poem appeared in his book *Nonsense Songs, Stories, Botany, and Botany*, which was published in 1871. In his poems he often invented words, like "runcible."

They dined on mince and slices of quince,
      Which they ate with a runcible spoon;
And hand in hand, on the edge of the sand,
      They danced by the light of the moon, the moon,
      They danced by the light of the moon.

–EDWARD LEAR

The Pobble Who Has No Toes

The Pobble who has no toes
     Had once as many as we;
When they said, "Some day you may lose them all,"
     He replied "Fish Fiddle-de-dee!"
And his Aunt Jobiska made him drink
Lavender water tinged with pink
For she said, "The world in general knows
There's nothing so good for a Pobble's toes!"

The Pobble who has no toes
     Swam across the Bristol Channel;
But before he set out he wrapped his nose
     In a piece of scarlet flannel.
For his Aunt Jobiska said, "No harm
Can come to his toes if his nose is warm;
And it's perfectly known that a Pobble's toes
Are safe—provided he minds his nose."

The Pobble swam fast and well,
     And when boats or ships came near him,
He tinkledy-blinkedy-winkled a bell,
     So that all the world could hear him,

And all the sailors and admirals cried,
When they saw him nearing the further side,
"He has gone to fish for his Aunt Jobiska's
Runcible Cat with crimson whiskers!"

Edward Lear had poor eyesight and suffered from epilepsy and asthma. He was a lonely man, often terribly depressed, and was convinced that those who met him were repelled by his ugliness. Many people, including the poet W.H. Auden, believe that he took refuge in the wonderful nonsense of his poems.

But before he touched the shore—
     The shore of the Bristol Channel—
A sea-green porpoise carried away
     His wrapper of scarlet flannel,
And when he came to observe his feet,
Formerly garnished with toes so neat,
His face at once became forlorn
On perceiving that all his toes were gone!

And nobody ever knew,
     From that dark day to the present,
Whoso had taken the Pobble's toes,
     In a manner so far from pleasant.
Whether the shrimps or crawfish gray,
Or crafty mermaids stole them away—
Nobody knew; and nobody knows
How the Pobble was robbed of his twice five toes!

The Pobble who has no toes
     Was placed in a friendly bark,
And they rowed him back, and carried him up
     To his Aunt Jobiska's park.
And she made him a feast, at his earnest wish,
Of eggs and buttercups fried with fish;
And she said, "It's a fact the whole world knows,
That Pobbles are happier without their toes."

—EDWARD LEAR

Mr. Nobody

I know a funny little man,
    As quiet as a mouse,
Who does the mischief that is done
    In everybody's house!
There's no one ever sees his face,
    And yet we all agree
That every plate we break was cracked
    By Mr. Nobody.

'Tis he who always tears our books,
    Who leaves the door ajar,
He pulls the buttons from our shirts,
    And scatters pins afar;
That squeaking door will always squeak,
    For, prithee, don't you see,
We leave the oiling to be done
    By Mr. Nobody.

The finger marks upon the door
    By none of us are made;
We never leave the blinds unclosed,
    To let the curtains fade.
The ink we never spill; the books
    That lying round you see
Are not our books—they all belong
    To Mr. Nobody.

—AUTHOR UNKNOWN

Three Blind Mice

THE WHOLE STORY

Three small mice,
Three small mice,
    Pined for some fun,
    Pined for some fun.
They made up their minds to set out to roam;
Said they, "'Tis dull to remain at home,"
And all the luggage they took was a comb,
    These three small mice.

Three bold mice,
Three bold mice,
    Came to an inn,
    Came to an inn.
"Good evening, Host, can you give us a bed?"
But the host he grinned and he shook his head,
So they all slept out in a field instead,
    These three bold mice.

Three cold mice,
Three cold mice,
    Woke up next morn,
    Woke up next morn,
They each had a cold and a swollen face,
Through sleeping all night in an open space,
So they rose quite early and left the place,
    These three cold mice.

Three hungry mice,
Three hungry mice,

Everyone, or nearly everyone, knows the little ditty about the three blind mice. But not many people know how they lost their sight, why the farmer's wife cut off their tails, and what happened to them after that. This poem tells the whole story of the three little mice. It can be sung or recited.

Searched for some food,

Searched for some food,

But all they found was a walnut shell

That lay by the side of a dried-up well.

Who had eaten the nut they could not tell,

These three hungry mice.

Three starved mice,

Three starved mice,

Came to a farm,

Came to a farm,

The farmer was eating some bread and cheese;

So they all went down on thier hands and knees,

And squeaked, "Pray, give us a morsel, please,"

These three starved mice.

Three glad mice,

Three glad mice,

Ate all they could,

Ate all they could.

They felt so happy they danced with glee;

But the farmer's wife came in to see

What might this merrymaking be

Of three glad mice.

Three poor mice,

Three poor mice,

Soon changed their tone,

Soon changed their tone.

The farmer's wife said, "What are you at,

And why were you capering round like that?

Just wait a minute: I'll fetch the cat."
  Oh, dear! poor mice.

  Three scared mice,
  Three scared mice,
    Ran for their lives,
    Ran for their lives,
They jumped out onto the window ledge;
The mention of "cat" set their teeth on edge,
So they hid themselves in the bramble hedge,
  These three scared mice.

  Three sad mice,
  Three sad mice,
    What could they do?
    What could they do?
The bramble hedge was most unkind:
It scratched their eyes and made them blind,
And soon each mouse went out of his mind,
  These three sad mice.

  Three blind mice,
  Three blind mice,
    See how they run!
    See how they run!
They all ran after the farmer's wife,
Who cut off their tails with the carving knife.
Did you ever see such a sight in your life
  As three blind mice?

  Three sick mice,
  Three sick mice,

Gave way to tears,

Gave way to tears.

They could not see and they had no end;

They sought a doctor and found a friend.

He gave them some "Never too late to mend,"

These three sick mice.

Three wise mice,

Three wise mice,

Rubbed rubbed away,

Rubbed rubbed away,

And soon their tails began to grow,

And their eyes recovered their sight, you know;

They looked in the glass and it told them so,

These three wise mice.

Three proud mice,

Three proud mice,

Soon settled down,

Soon settled down.

The name of their house I cannot tell,

But they've learned a trade and are doing well.

If you call upon them, ring the bell

Three times twice.

—JOHN W. IVIMEY

The Letters at School

One day the letters went to school,
    And tried to learn each other;
They got so mixed 't was really hard
    To pick out one from t' other.

A went in first, and Z went last;
    The rest all were between them—
K, L, and M, and N, O, P—
    I wish you could have seen them!

B, C, D, E, and J, K, L,
    Soon jostled well their betters;
Q, R, S, T—I grieve to say—
    Were very naughty letters.

Of course, ere long, they came to words—
    What else could be expected?
Till E made D, J, C, and T
    Decidedly dejected.

Now, through it all, the Consonants
    Were rudest and uncouthest,
While all the pretty Vowel girls
    Were certainly the smoothest.

And simple U kept far from Q,
    With face demure and moral,
"Because," she said, "we are, we two,
    So apt to start a quarrel!"

Mary Mapes Dodge, who wrote this amusing poem, is best-known as the author of *Hans Brinker*; or *The Silver Skates*, a book much loved by children since it was first published more than one hundred years ago. Ms. Dodge was also the first editor of *St. Nicholas*, an extremely popular children's magazine.

But spiteful P said, "Pooh for U!"
　　　(Which made her feel quite bitter),
And, calling O, L, E to help,
　　　He really tried to hit her.

Cried A, "Now E and C, come here!
　　　If both will aid a minute,
Good P will join in making peace,
　　　Or else the mischief's in it."

And smiling E, the ready sprite,
　　　Said, "Yes, and count me double."
This done, sweet peace shone o'er the scene,
　　　And gone was all the trouble!

Meanwhile, when U and P made up,
　　　The Cons'nants looked about them,
And kissed the Vowels, for, you see,
　　　They could not do without them.

–MARY MAPES DODGE

Jabberwocky

'Twas brllig, and the slithy toves,
      Did gyre and gimble in the wabe;
All mimsy were the borogoves,
      And the mome raths outgrabe.

"Beware the Jabberwock, my son!
      The jaws that bite, the claws that catch!
Beware the Jubjub bird, and shun
      The frumious Bandersnatch!"

He took his vorpal sword in hand:
      Long time the manxome foe he sought.—
So rested he by the Tumtum tree,
      And stood awhile in thought.

And as in uffish thought he stood,
      The Jabberwock, with eyes of flame,
Came whiffling through the tulgey wood,
      And burbled as it came!

One, two! One, two! And through and through
      The vorpal blade went snicker-snack!
He left it dead, and with its head
      He went galumphing back.

"And hast thou slain the Jabberwock?
      Come to my arms, my beamish boy!
O frabjous day! Callooh! Callay!"
      He chortled in his joy.

In the first chapter of *Through the Looking-Glass*, the sequel to *Alice in Wonderland*, Alice picks up a book with reversed printing and, by holding it up to the mirror she has just passed through, she reads this poem.

'Twas brillig, and the slithy toves
      Did gyre and gimble in the wabe;
All mimsy were the borogoves,
      And the mome raths outgrabe.

–LEWIS CARROLL

EARTH AND SKY

The snow, the rain, the wind, a rainbow, daffodils, a tree in bloom,

the sunset, and the moon have all inspired poets. After all, it is these wonders

of nature that bring beauty into our lives, affect our moods, even force us to

change our plans. In this section some of the world's finest poets celebrate

the changing seasons and nature's magic that is everywhere.

The Cloud

I bring fresh showers for the thirsting flowers,
  From the seas and the streams;
I bear light shade for the leaves when laid
  In their noonday dreams.
From my wings are shaken the dews that waken
  The sweet buds every one,
When rocked to rest on their mother's breast,
  As she dances about the sun.
I wield the flail of the lashing hail,
  And whiten the green plains under;
And then again I dissolve it in rain,
  And laugh as I pass in thunder.

–PERCY BYSSHE SHELLEY

Percy Bysshe Shelley, who was only thirty when he died, was one of England's great Romantic poets. He believed that poetry "awakens and enlarges the mind," lifting "the veil from the hidden beauty of the world."

The Months

January cold and desolate;
February dripping wet;
March wind ranges;
April changes;
Birds sing in tune
To flowers of May,
And sunny June
Brings longest day;
In scorched July
The storm clouds fly,
Lightning-torn;
August bears corn,
September fruit;
In rough October
Earth must disrobe her;
Stars fall and shoot
In keen November;
And night is long
And cold is strong
In bleak December.

–CHRISTINA ROSSETTI

February Twilight

I stood beside a hill
    Smooth with new-laid snow,
A single star looked out
    From the cold evening glow.

There was no other creature
    That saw what I could see—
I stood and watched the evening star
    As long as it watched me.

—SARA TEASDALE

Sara Teasdale was born in St. Louis and educated at home and in private schools. She won a special Pulitzer Prize for *Love Songs*, a book of poetry. She also wrote poems for children that were collected in two volumes.

The Storm

See lightning is flashing,
The forest is crashing,
The rain will come dashing,
    A flood will be rising anon;

The heavens are scowling,
The thunder is growling,
The loud winds are howling,
    The storm has come suddenly on!

But now the sky clears,
The bright sun appears,
Now nobody fears,
    But soon every cloud will be gone.

–SARA COLERIDGE

Who Has Seen the Wind?

Who has seen the wind?
    Neither I nor you:
But when the leaves hang trembling,
    The wind is passing through.

Who has seen the wind?
    Neither you nor I:
But when the leaves bow down their heads,
    The wind is passing by.

–CHRISTINA ROSSETTI

Trees

I think that I shall never see
A poem lovely as a tree.

A tree whose hungry mouth is pressed
Against the earth's sweet flowing breast;

A tree that looks at God all day
And lifts her leafy arms to pray;

A tree that may in summer wear
A nest of robins in her hair;

Upon whose bosom snow has lain;
Who intimately lives with rain.

Poems are made by fools like me,
But only God can make a tree.

–JOYCE KILMER

Joyce Kilmer, who was born in New Brunswick, New Jersey, died under German gunfire on July 30, 1918, in the second Battle of the Marne during World War I. This poem, his most popular, first appeared in *Poetry* magazine when he was on the staff of *The New York Times Review of Books*. It is said that a white oak tree on the Rutgers University campus inspired the poem which his mother, Annie Kilmer, first set to music.

Trees

The oak is called the king of trees,
The aspen quivers in the breeze,
The poplar grows up straight and tall,
The peach tree spreads along the wall,
The sycamore gives pleasant shade,
The willow droops in watery glade,
The fir tree useful timber gives,
The beech amid the forest lives.

—SARA COLERIDGE

Blossoms

Out of my window I could see
But yesterday, upon the tree,
The blossoms white, like tufts of snow
That had forgotten when to go.

And while I looked out at them, they
Seemed like small butterflies at play,
For in the breeze their flutterings
Made me imagine them with wings.

I must have fancied well, for now
There's not a blossom on the bough,
And out of doors 't is raining fast,
And gusts of wind are whistling past.

With butterflies 't is etiquette
To keep their wings from getting wet,
So, when they knew the storm was near,
They thought it best to disappear.

—FRANK DEMPSTER SHERMAN

Frank Dempster Sherman, who was a professor of architecture and graphics at Columbia University, had many of his poems published in *St. Nicholas* and other children's magazines.

The Wind

I saw you toss the kites on high
And blow the birds about the sky,
And all around I heard you pass,
Like ladies' skirts across the grass—
      O wind, a-blowing all day long,
      O wind, that sings so loud a song!

I saw the different things you did,
But always you yourself you hid.
I felt you push, I heard you call,
I could not see yourself at all—
      O wind, a-blowing all day long,
      O wind, that sings so loud a song!

O you that are so strong and cold,
O blower, are you young or old?
Are you a beast of field and tree,
Or just a stronger child than me?
      O wind, a-blowing all day long,
      O wind, that sings so loud a song!

–ROBERT LOUIS STEVENSON

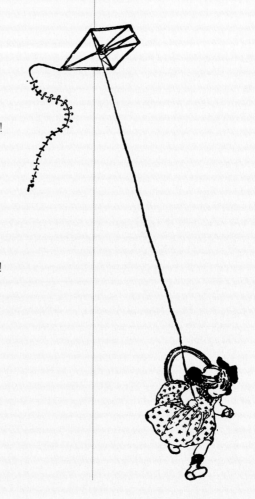

The Snowflake

Before I melt,
Come, look at me!
This lovely icy filigree!
Of a great forest
In one night
I make a wilderness
Of white:
By skyey cold
Of crystals made,
All softly, on
Your finger laid,
I pause, that you
My beauty see:
Breathe; and I vanish
Instantly.

—WALTER DE LA MARE

Rain

More than the wind, more than the snow,
More than the sunshine, I love rain;
Whether it droppeth soft and low
Whether it rusheth amain.

Dark as the night it spreadeth its wings,
Slow and silently up on the hills;
Then sweeps o'er the vale, like a steel that springs
From the grasp of a thousand wills.

Swift sweeps under heaven the raven cloud's flight;
And the land and the lakes and the main
Lie belted beneath with steel-bright light,
The light of the swift-rushing rain.

On evening of summer, when sunlight is low,
Soft the rain falls from opal-hued skies;
And the flowers the most delicate summer can show
Are not stirr'd by its gentle surprise.

It falls on the pools, and no wrinkling it makes,
But touching melts in, like the smile
That sinks in the face of a dreamer, but breaks
Not the calm of his dream's happy wile.

The grass rises up as it falls on the meads,
The bird softlier sings in his bower,
And the circles of gnats circle on like wing'd seeds
Through the soft sunny lines of the shower.

—EBENEZEER JONES

August

Buttercup nodded and said good-bye.
Clover and daisy went off together,
But the fragrant water lilies lie
Yet moored in the golden August weather.

The swallows chatter about their flight,
The cricket chirps like a rare good fellow,
The asters twinkle in clusters bright,
While the corn grows ripe and the apples mellow.

—CELIA THAXTER

Spring

Sound the flute!
Now it's mute.
Birds delight
Day and night;
Nightingale
In the dale,
Lark in the sky—
Merrily,
Merrily, merrily to welcome in the year.

Little boy,
Full of joy;
Little girl,
Sweet and small;
Cock does crow,
So do you
Merry voice,
Infant noise,
Merrily, merrily, to welcome in the year.

Little lamb,
Here I am;
Come and lick
My white neck;
Let me pull
Your soft wool;
Let me kiss
Your soft face;
Merrily, merrily, we welcome in the year.

–WILLIAM BLAKE

I Heard a Bird Sing

I heard a bird sing
        In the dark of December
A magical thing
        And sweet to remember.

"We are nearer to spring
        Than we were in September,"
I heard a bird sing
        In the dark of December.

—OLIVER HERFORD

The Daffodils

I wandered lonely as a cloud
That floats on high o'er vales and hills,
When all at once I saw a crowd,
A host, of golden daffodils;
Beside the lake, beneath the trees,
Fluttering and dancing in the breeze.

Continuous as the stars that shine
And twinkle on the milky way,
They stretched in never-ending line
Along the margin of a bay:
Ten thousand saw I at a glance,
Tossing their heads in sprightly dance.

The waves beside them danced; but they
Outdid the sparkling waves in glee:
A poet could not but be gay,
In such a jocund company:
I gazed—and gazed—but little thought
What wealth the show to me had brought:

For oft, when on my couch I lie
In vacant or in pensive mood,
They flash upon that inward eye
Which is the bliss of solitude;
And then my heart with pleasure fills,
And dances with the daffodils.

—WILLIAM WORDSWORTH

William Wordsworth was inspired to write this poem after a walk in the woods with his younger sister, Dorothy. She described the scene in her journal: "I never saw daffodils so beautiful. They grew among the mossy stones, about and above them; some rested their head on these stones as on a pillow for weariness; and the rest tossed, and reeled, and danced, and seemed as if they laughed with the wind that blew upon them over the lake. They looked so gay, ever glancing, ever changing."

September

The goldenrod is yellow;
      The corn is turning brown;
The trees in apple orchards
      With fruit are bending down.

The gentian's bluest fringes
      Are curling in the sun;
In dusty pods the milkweed
      Its hidden silk has spun.

The sedges flaunt their harvest
      In every meadow nook;
And asters by the brook-side
      Make asters in the brook.

From dewy lanes at morning
      The grapes' sweet odors rise;
At noon the roads all flutter
      With yellow butterflies.

By all these lovely tokens
      September days are here,
With summer's best of weather,
      And autumn's best of cheer.

—HELEN HUNT JACKSON

Helen Hunt Jackson was a novelist, poet, and a crusader for the rights of Native Americans. Born in Amherst, Massachusetts, she was a friend and schoolmate of Emily Dickinson. After she married she settled in Colorado Springs. She contributed poems to many magazines, wrote travel books, children's books, and the much-admired novel, *Ramona*.

JESSIE WILLCOX SMITH

November

The leaves are fading and falling,
    The winds are rough and wild,
The birds have ceased their calling,
    But let me tell you, my child,

Though day by day, as it closes,
    Doth darker and colder grow,
The roots of the bright red roses
    Will keep alive in the snow.

And when the winter is over,
    The boughs will get new leaves,
The quail come back to the clover,
    And the swallow back to the eaves.

The robin will wear on his bosom
    A vest that is bright and new,
And the loveliest wayside blossom
    Will shine with the sun and dew.

The leaves today are whirling,
    The brooks are dry and dumb,
But let me tell you, my darling,
    That spring will be sure to come.

There must be rough, cold weather,
    And winds and rains so wild;
Not all good things together
    Come to us here, my child.

Alice Cary was born on a farm near Cincinnati, Ohio, the fourth of nine children. Although they went to school for only a few years, she and her sister, Phoebe, published their first book of poems when she was thirty. She moved to New York with her sister and within six years they had earned enough money from their writing to buy a house. They were both active in the struggle for women's rights.

So, when some dear joy loses
   Its beauteous summer glow,
Think how the roots of the roses
   Are kept alive in the snow.

–ALICE CARY

Fog

The fog comes
on little cat feet.

It sits looking
over harbor and city
on silver haunches
and then moves on.

–CARL SANDBURG

The Star

Twinkle, twinkle, little star,
How I wonder what you are!
Up above the world so high,
Like a diamond in the sky.

When the blazing sun is gone,
When he nothing shines upon,
Then you show your little light,
Twinkle, twinkle, all the night.

Then the traveler in the dark,
Thanks you for your tiny spark,
He could not see which way to go
If you did not twinkle so.

In the dark blue sky you keep,
And often through my curtains peep,
For you never shut your eye,
'Til the sun is in the sky.

As your bright and tiny spark
Lights the traveler in the dark—
Though I know not what you are,
Twinkle, twinkle, little star.

—JANE TAYLOR

Jane Taylor and her sister, Ann, wrote many poems for adults as well as for children. Born in London, Jane wrote this well-known verse in the early nineteenth century. Although many poems about the stars have been written, this is, undoubtedly, the most famous and beloved.

Silver

Slowly, silently, now the moon
Walks the night in her silver shoon;
This way, and that, she peers, and sees
Silver fruit upon silver trees;
One by one the casements catch
Her beams beneath the silver thatch;
Couched in his kennel, like a log,
With paws of silver sleeps the dog;
From their shadowy cote the white breasts peep
Of doves in a silver-feathered sleep;
A harvest mouse goes scampering by,
With silver claws, and silver eye;
And moveless fish in the water gleam,
By silver reeds in a silver stream.

—WALTER DE LA MARE

The Moon's the North Wind's Cookie

WHAT THE LITTLE GIRL SAID

The Moon's the North Wind's cookie,
He bites it day by day,
Until there's but a rim of scraps
That crumble all away.

The South Wind is a baker
He kneads clouds in his den,
And bakes a crisp new moon that . . . greedy
North . . . Wind . . . eats . . . again!

–VACHEL LINDSAY

POEMS THAT TELL STORIES

Many of the poems in this section are quite long. A few of them are funny, a couple are mysterious. Some tell true stories, others are fables. Many of them are written by famous poets, including Henry Wadsworth Longfellow and Robert Browning. Several of them, like "A Visit from St. Nicholas" and the story of the Pied Piper may be familiar to you. But all these tales have one thing in common—they are all wonderful poems.

Hiawatha's Childhood

By the shores of Gitchie Gumee,
By the shining Big-Sea-Water,
Stood the wigwam of Nokimis,
Daughter of the Moon, Nokomis.
Dark behind it rose the forest,
Rose the black and gloomy pine trees,
Rose the firs with cones upon them;
Bright before it beat the water,
Beat the clear and sunny water,
Beat the shining Big-Sea-Water.
      There the wrinkled old Nokomis
Nursed the little Hiawatha,
Rocked him in his linden cradle,
Bedded soft in moss and rushes,
Safely bound with reindeer sinews;
Stilled his fretful wail by saying,
"Hush! the Naked Bear will hear thee!"
Lulled him into slumber, singing,
"Ewa-yea! my little owlet!
Who is this, that lights the wigwam?
With his great eyes lights the wigwam?
Ewa-yea! my little owlet!"
      Many things Nokomis taught him
Of the stars that shine in heaven;
Showed him Ishkoodah, the comet,
Ishkoodah, with fiery tresses;
Showed the Death-Dance of the spirits,
Warriors with their plumes and war clubs,

Hiawatha, which means "He Makes Rivers," was a legendary chief of the Onondaga tribe of North American Indians. According to Indian tradition, in the fifteenth century Hiawatha formed the League of Five Nations, known as the Iroquois. Henry Wadsworth Longfellow celebrated his life in a long poem, "The Song of Hiawatha" of which this is the first section. Longfellow wrote the poem in trochaic tetrameters, which capture the rhythm of tom toms.

Flaring far away to northward
In the frosty nights of winter;
Showed the broad white road in heaven,
Pathway of the ghosts, the shadows,
Running straight across the heavens,
Crowded with the ghosts, the shadows.

    At the door on summer evenings,
Sat the little Hiawatha;
Heard the whispering of the pine trees,
Heard the lapping of the waters,
Sounds of music, words of wonder;
"Minne-wawa!" said the pine trees,
"Mudway-aushka!" said the water.

    Saw the firefly Wah-wah-taysee,
Flitting through the dusk of evening,
With the twinkle of its candle
Lighting up the brakes and bushes,
And he sang the song of children,
Sang the song Nokomis taught him:
"Wah-wah-taysee, little firefly,
Little, flitting, white-fire insect,
Little, dancing, white-fire creature,
Light me with your little candle,
Ere upon my bed I lay me,
Ere in sleep I close my eyelids!"

    Saw the moon rise from the water,
Rippling, rounding from the water,
Saw the flecks and shadows on it,
Whispered, "What is that, Nokomis?"
And the good Nokomis answered:

"Once a warrior, very angry,
Seized his grandmother, and threw her
Up into the sky at midnight;
'Tis her body that you see there."
          Saw the rainbow in the heaven,
In the eastern sky the rainbow,
Whispered, "What is that, Nokomis?"
And the good Nokomis answered:
"'Tis the heaven of flowers you see there;
All the wild flowers of the forest,
All the lilies of the prairie,
When on earth they fade and perish,
Blossom in that heaven above us."
          When he heard the owls at midnight,
Hooting, laughing in the forest,
"What is that?" he cried in terror;
"What is that," he said, "Nokomis?"
And the good Nokomis answered:
"That is but the owl and owlet,

Talking in their native language,
Talking, scolding at each other."
   Then the little Hiawatha
Learned of every bird its language,
Learned their names and all their secrets,
How they built their nests in summer,
Where they hid themselves in winter,
Talked with them when e'er he met them,
Called them "Hiawatha's Chickens."
Of all beasts he learned the language,
Learned their names and all their secrets,
How the beavers built their lodges,
Where the squirrels hid their acorns,
How the reindeer ran so swiftly,
Why the rabbit was so timid,
Talked with them whene'er he met them,
Called them "Hiawatha's Brothers."

–HENRY WADSWORTH LONGFELLOW

Casey at the Bat

The outlook wasn't brilliant for the Mudville nine that day;
The score stood four to two with but one inning more to play.
And then when Cooney died at first, and Barrows did the same,
A sickly silence fell upon the patrons of the game.

A straggling few got up to go in deep despair. The rest
Clung to that hope which springs eternal in the human breast;
They thought if only Casey could but get a whack at that—
We'd put up even money now with Casey at the bat.

This is certainly the greatest poem about baseball that has ever been written. There have even been several film versions. Its author, Ernest Lawrence Thayer, had a humor column in a San Francisco newspaper and it was in that column, on Sunday, June 3, 1888, that Casey first appeared.

But Flynn preceded Casey, as did also Jimmy Blake,
And the former was a lulu and the latter was a cake;
So upon that stricken multitude grim melancholy sat,
For there seemed but little chance of Casey's getting to the bat.

But Flynn let drive a single, to the wonderment of all,
And Blake, the much despis-ed, tore the cover off the ball;
And when the dust had lifted, and the men saw what had occurred,
There was Johnnie safe at second and Flynn a-hugging third.

Then from five thousand throats and more there rose a lusty yell;
It rumbled through the valley, it rattled in the dell;
It knocked upon the mountain and recoiled upon the flat,
For Casey, mighty Casey, was advancing to the bat.

There was ease in Casey's manner as he stepped into his place;
There was pride in Casey's bearing and a smile on Casey's face.
And when, responding to the cheers, he lightly doffed his hat,
No stranger in the crowd could doubt 'twas Casey at the bat.

Ten thousand eyes were on him as he rubbed his hands with dirt;
Five thousand tongues applauded when he wiped them on his shirt.
Then while the writhing pitcher ground the ball into his hip,
Defiance gleamed in Casey's eye, a sneer curled Casey's lip.

And now the leather-covered sphere came hurtling through the air,
And Casey stood a-watching it in haughty grandeur there.
Close by the sturdy batsman the ball unheeded sped—
"That ain't my style," said Casey. "Strike one," the umpire said.

From the benches, black with people, there went up a muffled roar,
Like the beating of the storm-waves on a stern and distant shore.

"Kill him! Kill the umpire!" shouted someone on the stand;
And it's likely they'd have killed him had not Casey raised his hand.

With a smile of Christian charity great Casey's visage shone;
He stilled the rising tumult; he bade the game go on;
He signaled to the pitcher, and once more the spheroid flew;
But Casey still ignored it, and the umpire said, "Strike two."

"Fraud!" cried the maddened thousands, and echo answered fraud;
But one scornful look from Casey and the audience was awed.
They saw his face grow stern and cold, they saw his muscles strain,
And they knew that Casey wouldn't let that ball go by again.

The sneer is gone from Casey's lip, his teeth are clenched in hate;
He pounds with cruel violence his bat upon the plate.
And now the pitcher holds the ball, and now he lets it go,
And now the air is shattered by the force of Casey's blow.

Oh, somewhere in this favored land the sun is shining bright;
The band is playing somewhere, and somewhere hearts are light,
And somewhere men are laughing, and somewhere children shout;
But there is no joy in Mudville—mighty Casey has struck out.

–ERNEST LAWRENCE THAYER

Paul Revere's Ride

Listen, my children, and you shall hear
Of the midnight ride of Paul Revere,
On the eighteenth of April, in Seventy-five;
Hardly a man is now alive
Who remembers that famous day and year.

He said to his friend, "If the British march
By land or sea from the town tonight,
Hang a lantern aloft in the belfry arch
Of the North Church tower as a signal light—
One, if by land, and two, if by sea;
And I on the opposite shore will be,
Ready to ride and spread the alarm
Through every Middlesex village and farm,
For the country folk to be up and to arm."

Then he said, "Good night" and with muffled oar
Silently rowed to the Charlestown shore,
Just as the moon rose over the bay,
Where swinging wide at her moorings lay
The *Somerset*, British man-of-war;
A phantom ship, with each mast and spar
Across the moon like a prison bar,
And a huge black hulk, that was magnified
By its own reflection in the tide.

Meanwhile, his friend, through alley and street,
Wanders and watches, with eager ears,
Till in the silence around him he hears
The muster of men at the barrack door,

Paul Revere, a silversmith and an engraver, was one of many couriers working for the rebels during the American Revolution. Although the poem is inaccurate in some of the historical details, Revere did make his ride on April 18, 1775. It would not have been remembered if Henry Wadsworth Longfellow had not written about it.

The sound of arms, and the tramp of feet,
And the measured tread of the grenadiers,
Marching down to their boats on the shore.

Then he climbed to the tower of the Old North Church,
By the wooden stairs, with stealthy tread,
To the belfry-chamber overhead,
And startled the pigeons from their perch
On the somber rafters, that round him made
Masses and moving shapes of shade—
By the trembling ladder, steep and tall,
To the highest window in the wall,
Where he paused to listen and look down
A moment on the roofs of the town,
And the moonlight flowing over all.

Beneath, in the churchyard, lay the dead,
In their night-encampment on the hill,
Wrapped in silence so deep and still
That he could hear, like a sentinel's tread,
The watchful night wind, as it went
Creeping along from tent to tent,
And seeming to whisper, "All is well!"
A moment only he feels the spell
Of the place and the hour, and the secret dread
Of the lonely belfry and the dead;
For suddenly all his thoughts are bent
On a shadowy something far away,
Where the river widens to meet the bay—
A line of black that bends and floats
On the rising tide, like a bridge of boats.

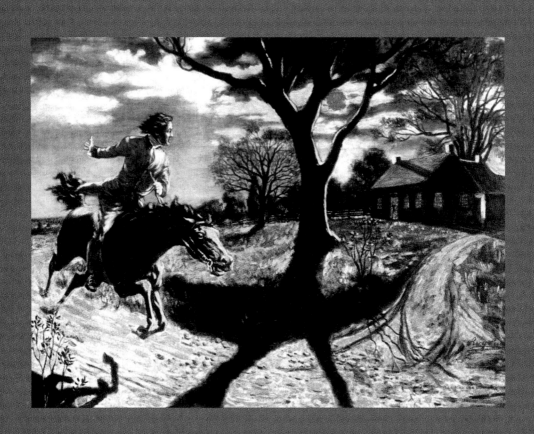

Meanwhile, impatient to mount and ride,
Booted and spurred, with a heavy stride
On the opposite shore walked Paul Revere.
Now he patted his horse's side,
Now gazed at the landscape far and near,
Then, impetuous, stamped the earth,
And turned and tightened his saddle girth;
But mostly he watched with eager search
The belfry tower of the Old North Church,
As it rose above the graves on the hill,
Lonely and spectral and somber and still.
And lo! as he looks, on the belfry's height
A glimmer, and then a gleam of light!
He springs to the saddle, the bridle he turns,
But lingers and gazes, till full on his sight
A second lamp in the belfry burns!

A hurry of hoofs in a village street,
A shape in the moonlight, a bulk in the dark,
And beneath, from the pebbles, in passing, a spark
Struck out by a steed flying fearless and fleet:
That was all! And yet, through the gloom and the light,
The fate of a nation was riding that night;
And the spark struck out by that steed, in his flight,
Kindled the land into flame with its heat.
He has left the village and mounted the steep,
And beneath him, tranquil and broad and deep,
Is the Mystic, meeting the ocean tides;
And under the alders that skirt its edge,
Now soft on the sand, now loud on the ledge,
Is heard the tramp of his steed as he rides.

It was twelve by the village clock,
When he crossed the bridge into Medford town.
He heard the crowing of the cock,
And the barking of the farmer's dog,
And felt the damp of the river fog,
That rises after the sun goes down.

It was one by the village clock,
When he galloped into Lexington.
He saw the gilded weathercock
Swim in the moonlight as he passed,
And the meeting-house windows, blank and bare,
Gaze at him with a spectral glare,
As if they already stood aghast
At the bloody work they would look upon.

It was two by the village clock,
When he came to the bridge in Concord town.
He heard the bleating of the flock,
And the twitter of birds among the trees,
And felt the breath of the morning breeze
Blowing over the meadows brown.
And one was safe and asleep in his bed
Who at the bridge would be first to fall,
Who that day would be lying dead,
Pierced by a British musket-ball.

You know the rest. In the books you have read
How the British Regulars fired and fled—
How the farmers gave them ball for ball,
From behind each fence and farmyard wall,

Chasing the redcoats down the lane,
Then crossing the fields to emerge again
Under the trees at the turn of the road,
And only pausing to fire and load.

So through the night rode Paul Revere;
And so through the night went his cry of alarm
To every Middlesex village and farm—
A cry of defiance and not of fear,
A voice in the darkness, a knock at the door,
And a word that shall echo forevermore!
For, borne on the night wind of the Past,
Through all our history, to the last,
In the hour of darkness and peril and need,
The people will awaken and listen to hear
The hurrying hoofbeats of that steed,
And the midnight message of Paul Revere.

–HENRY WADSWORTH LONGFELLOW

The Spider and the Fly

A FABLE

"Will you walk into my parlor?" said the spider to the fly;
"'Tis the prettiest little parlor that ever you did spy.
The way into my parlor is up a winding stair,
And I have many pretty things to show when you are there."

"O no, no," said the little fly, "to ask me is in vain
"For who goes up your winding stair can ne'er come down again."

"I'm sure you must be weary, dear, with soaring up so high;
Will you rest upon my little bed?" said the spider to the fly.
"There are pretty curtains drawn around, the sheets are fine and thin,
And if you like to rest awhile, I'll snugly tuck you in."

"O no, no," said the little fly, "for I've often heard it said,
They never, never wake again, who sleep upon your bed."

Said the cunning spider to the fly, "Dear friend, what shall I do,
To prove the warm affection I've always felt for you?
I have within my pantry good store of all that's nice;
I'm sure you're very welcome; will you please to take a slice?"

"O no, no," said the little fly, "kind sir, that cannot be;
I've heard what's in your pantry, and I do not wish to see."

"Sweet creature!" said the spider, "you're witty and you're wise.
How handsome are your gauzy wings, how brilliant are your eyes!
I have a little looking-glass upon my parlor shelf,
If you'll step in one moment, dear, you shall behold yourself."

"I thank you, gentle sir," she said, "for what you're pleased to say,
And bidding you good morning soon, I'll call another day."

The spider turned him round about, and went into his den,
For well he knew the silly fly would soon be back again:
So he wove a subtle web, in a little corner sly,
And set his table ready to dine upon the fly.
Then he came out to his door again, and merrily did sing,
"Come hither, hither, pretty fly, with the pearl and silver wing:
Your robes are green and purple; there's a crest upon your head;
Your eyes are like the diamond bright, but mine are dull as lead."

Alas, alas! how very soon this silly little fly,
Hearing his wily flattering words, came slowly flitting by.
With buzzing wings she hung aloft, then near and nearer drew,
Thinking only of her brilliant eyes, and green and purple hue;
Thinking only of her crested head—poor foolish thing! At last,
Up jumped the cunning spider, and fiercely held her fast.
He dragged her up his winding stair, into his dismal den,
Within his little parlor; but she ne'er came out again!

And now, dear little children, who may this story read,
To idle, silly, flattering words, I pray you ne'er give heed;
Unto an evil counselor close heart, and ear, and eye,
And take a lesson from this tale of the spider and the fly.

—MARY HOWITT

Matilda Who Told Lies, and Was Burned to Death

Matilda told such dreadful lies,
It made one gasp and stretch one's eyes;
Her Aunt, who, from her earliest youth,
Had kept a strict regard for truth,
Attempted to believe Matilda:
The effort very nearly killed her,
And would have done so, had not she
Discovered this infirmity.
For once, toward the close of day,
Matilda, growing tired of play,
And finding she was left alone,
Went tiptoe to the telephone
And summoned the immediate aid
Of London's noble fire brigade.
Within an hour the gallant band
Were pouring in on every hand,
From Putney, Hackney Downs, and Bow
With courage high and hearts a-glow
They galloped, roaring through the town,
"Matilda's house is burning down!"
Inspired by British cheers and loud
Proceeding from the frenzied crowd,
They ran their ladders through a score
Of windows on the ballroom floor;
And took peculiar pains to souse
The pictures up and down the house,

This gruesome story is from Hilaire Belloc's book *Cautionary Tales*, which has been extremely popular with children since he wrote it more than one hundred years ago.

Until Matilda's Aunt succeeded
In showing them they were not needed;
And even then she had to pay
To get the men to go away!
It happened that a few weeks later
Her Aunt was off to the theater
To see that interesting play
The Second Mrs. Tanqueray,
She had refused to take her niece
To hear this entertaining piece:
A deprivation just and wise
To punish her for telling lies.
That night a fire did break out—
You should have heard Matilda shout!
You should have heard her scream and bawl,
And throw the window up and call
To people passing in the street—
(The rapidly increasing heat
Encouraging her to obtain
Their confidence)—but all in vain!
For every time she shouted "Fire!"
They only answered "Little liar!"
And therefore when her Aunt returned,
Matilda, and the house, were burned.

—HILAIRE BELLOC

The Pied Piper of Hamelin

A CHILD'S STORY

I

Hamelin Town's in Brunswick,
     By famous Hanover City;
The river Weser, deep and wide,
Washes its wall on the southern side;
A pleasanter spot you never spied;
     But, when begins my ditty,
Almost five hundred years ago,
To see the townsfolk suffer so
     From vermin, was a pity.

II

     Rats!
They fought the dogs and killed the cats,
     And bit the babies in the cradles,
And ate the cheeses out of the vats,
     And licked the soup from the cooks' own ladles,
Split open the kegs of salted sprats,
Made nests inside men's Sunday hats,
And even spoiled the women's chats
     By drowning their speaking
     With shrieking and squeaking
In fifty different sharps and flats.

III

At last the people in a body
     To the Town Hall came flocking:

Robert Browning was brought up with his only sister, Sarianna, in Camberwell in southeast London. His father, who worked for the Bank of England, had a library of more than six thousand books and it was here that Browning got most of his education. He wrote his first volume of poems when he was twelve years old, but his first published poem did not appear until nine years later. He dedicated this poem about the Pied Piper to "W.H. THE YOUNGER," who he addresses as "Willy" in the last stanza.

"'Tis clear," cried they, "our Mayor's a noddy;
        And as for our Corporation—shocking
To think we buy gowns lined with ermine
For dolts that can't or won't determine
What's best to rid us of our vermin!
You hope, because you're old and obese,
To find in the furry civic robe ease?
Rouse up, sirs! Give your brains a racking
To find the remedy we're lacking.
Or, sure as fate, we'll send you packing!"
At this the Mayor and corporation
Quaked with a might consternation.

IV

An hour they sat in council,
      At length the Mayor broke silence:
"For a guilder I'd my ermine gown sell,
      I wish I were a mile hence!
It's easy to bid one rack one's brain—
I'm sure my poor head aches again,
I've scratched it so, and all in vain.
Oh for a trap, a trap, a trap!"
Just as he said this, what should hap
At the chamber door but a gentle tap?
"Bless us," cried the Mayor, "what's this?"
(With the Corporation as he sat,
Looking little though wondrous fat;
Nor brighter was his eye, nor moister
Than a too-long-opened oyster,
Save when at noon his paunch grew mutinous
For a plate of turtle green and glutinous)
"Only a scraping of shoes on the mat?
Anything like the sound of a rat
Makes my heart go pit-a-pat!"

      V

"Come in!"—the Mayor cried, looking bigger:
And in did come the strangest figure!
His queer long coat from heel to head
Was half of yellow and half of red.
And he himself was tall and thin,
With sharp blue eyes, each like a pin,
With light loose hair, yet swarthy skin,
No tuft on cheek nor beard on chin.

But lips where smiles went out and in;
There was no guessing his kith and kin:
And nobody could enough admire
The tall man and his quaint attire.
Quoth one: "It's as my great-grandsire,
Starting up at the Trump of Doom's tone,
Had walked this way from his painted tombstone!"

VI

He advanced to the council table:
And, "Please your honors," said he, "I'm able,
By means of a secret charm, to draw
      All creatures living beneath the sun,
      That creep or swim or fly or run,
After me so as you never saw!
And I chiefly use my charm
On creatures that do people harm,
The mole and toad and newt and viper;
And people call me the Pied Piper."
(And here they noticed round his neck
      A scarf of red and yellow stripe,
To match with his coat of the selfsame check;
      And at the scarf's end a pipe;
And his fingers, they noticed, were ever straying
As if impatient to be playing
Upon this pipe, as low it dangled
Over his vesture so old-fangled.)
"Yet," said he, "poor piper as I am,
In Tartary I freed the Cham,
      Last June, from his huge swarms of gnats;
I eased in Asia the Nizam

Of a monstrous brood of vampire bats;
And as for what your brain bewilders,
If I can rid your town of rats
Will you give me a thousand guilders?"
"One? Fifty thousand!"—was the exclamation
Of the astonished Mayor and Corporation.

VII

Into the street the Piper stepped,
Smiling first a little smile,
As if he knew what magic slept
In his quiet pipe the while.
Then, like a musical adept,
To blow the pipe his lips he wrinkled,
And green and blue his sharp eyes twinkled,
Like a candle flame where salt is sprinkled;
And ere three shrill notes the pipe uttered,
You heard as if an army muttered;
And the muttering grew to a grumbling;
And the grumbling grew to a mighty rumbling;
And out of the houses the rats came tumbling.
Great rats, small rats, lean rats, brawny rats,
Brown rats, black rats, gray rats, tawny rats,
Grave old plodders, gay young friskers,
Fathers, mothers, uncles, cousins,
Cocking tails and pricking whiskers,
Families by tens and dozens,
Brothers, sisters, husbands, wives—
Followed the Piper for their lives.
From street to street he piped advancing,

And step for step they followed dancing,
Until they came to the river Weser,
  Wherein all plunged and perished!
—Save one who, stout as Julius Caesar,
Swam across and lived to carry
  (As he, the manuscript he cherished)
To Rat-land home his commentary:
Which was, "At the first shrill notes of the pipe,
I heard a sound as of scraping tripe,
And putting apples, wondrous ripe,
Into a cider press's gripe:
And a moving away of pickle tub-boards,
And a leaving ajar of conserve cupboards,
And a drawing the corks of train-oil flasks,
And a breaking the hoops of butter casks:
And it seemed as if a voice

(Sweeter far than by harp or by psaltery
Is breathed) called out, 'Oh rats, rejoice!
        The world is grown to one vast drysaltery!
So munch on, crunch one, take your nuncheon,
Breakfast, supper, dinner, luncheon!'
And just as a bulky sugar-puncheon,
All ready staved, like a great sun shone
Glorious scarce an inch before me,
Just as methought it said, 'Come, bore me!'
—I found the Weser rolling o'er me."

VIII

You should have heard the Hamelin people
Ringing the bells till they rocked the steeple.
"Go," cried the Mayor, "and get long poles,
Poke out the nests and block up the holes!
Consult with carpenters and builders,
And leave in our town not even a trace
Of the rats!"—when suddenly, up the face
Of the Piper perked in the marketplace,
With a "First, if you please, my thousand guilders!"

IX

A thousand guilders! The Major looked blue;
So did the Corporation, too.
For council dinners made rare havoc
With Claret, Moselle, Vin-de-Grave, Hock;
And half the money would replenish
Their cellar's biggest butt with Rhenish.
To pay this sum to a wandering fellow
With a gypsy coat of red and yellow!

"Beside," quoth the Mayor with a knowing wink,
"Our business was done at the river's brink;
We saw with our eyes the vermin sink,
And what's dead can't come to life, I think.
So, friend, we're not the folks to shrink
From the duty of giving you something for drink,
And a matter of money to put in your poke;
But as for the guilders, what we spoke
Of them, as you very well know, was in joke.
Beside, our losses have made us thrifty.
A thousand guilders! Come, take fifty!"

X

The Piper's face fell, and he cried
"No trifling! I can't wait, beside!
I've promised to visit by dinner time
Baghdad, and accept the prime
Of the head cook's pottage, all he's rich in,
For having left, in the Caliph's kitchen,
Of a nest of scorpions no survivor:
With him I proved no bargain-driver.
With you don't think I'll bate a stiver!
And folks who put me in a passion
May find me pipe after another fashion."

XI

"How?" cried the Mayor, "d'ye think I brook
Being worse treated than a Cook?
Insulted by a lazy ribald
With idle pipe and vesture piebald?

You threaten us, fellow? Do your worst,
Blow your pipe there till you burst!"

XII

Once more he stepped into the street
          And to his lips again
          Laid his long pipe of smooth straight cane;
And ere he blew three notes (such sweet
Soft notes as yet musician's cunning
          Never gave the enraptured air)
There was a rustling that seemed like a bustling
Of merry crowds jostling and pitching and hustling,
Small feet were pattering, wooden shoes clattering,
Little hands clapping and little tongues chattering,
And, like the fowls in a farmyard when barley is scattering,
Out came the children running.
All the little boys and girls,
With rose cheeks and flaxen curls,
And sparkling eyes and teeth like pearls,
Tripping and skipping, ran merrily after
The wonderful music with shouting and laughter.

XIII

The Mayor was dumb, and the Council stood
As if they were changed into blocks of wood.
Unable to move a step, or cry
To the children merrily skipping by,
—Could only follow with the eye
That joyous crowd at the Piper's back.
But now the Mayor was on the rack,
And the wretched Council's bosoms beat,

As the Piper turned from the High Street
To where the Weser rolled its waters
Right in the way of their sons and daughters!
However he turned from South to West,
And to Koppelberg Hill his steps addressed,
And after him the children pressed;
Great was the joy in every breast.
"He never can cross that mighty top!
He's forced to let the piping drop,
And we shall see our children stop!"
When, lo, as they reached the mountainside,
A wondrous portal opened wide,
As if a cavern was suddenly hollowed;
And the Piper advanced and the children followed,
And when all were in to the very last,
The door in the mountainside shut fast.
Did I say, all? No! One was lame,
      And could not dance the whole of the way;
And in after years, if you would blame
      His sadness, he was used to say—
"It's dull in our town since my playmates left!
I can't forget that I'm bereft
Of all the pleasant sights they see,
Which the Piper also promised me.
For he led us, he said, to a joyous land,
Joining the town and just at hand,
Where waters gushed and fruit trees grew
And flowers put forth a fairer hue,
And everything was strange and new;
The sparrows were brighter than peacocks here,

And their dogs outran our fallow deer,
And honeybees had lost their stings,
And horses were born with eagles' wings:
And just as I became assured
My lame foot would be speedily cured,
The music stopped and I stood still,
And found myself outside the hill,
Left alone against my will,
To go now limping as before,
And never hear of that country more!"

XIV

Alas, alas for Hamelin!
   There came into many a burgher's pate
   A text which says that heaven's gate
   Opens to the rich at as easy rate
As the needle's eye takes a camel in!
The Mayor sent East, West, North, and South,
To offer the Piper, by word of mouth,
   Wherever it was men's lot to find him,
Silver and gold to his heart's content,
If he'd only return the way he went,
   And bring the children behind him.
And when they saw 'twas a lost endeavor,
And Piper and dancers were gone forever,
They made a decree that lawyers never
   Should think their records dated duly
If, after the day of the month and year,
These words did not as well appear,
"And so long after what happened here
   On the Twenty-second of July,
Thirteen hundred and seventy-six":
And the better in memory to fix
The place of the children's last retreat,
They called it, the Pied Piper's Street—
Where anyone playing on pipe or tabor
Was sure for the future to lose his labor.
Nor suffered they hostelry or tavern
   To shock with mirth a street so solemn;
But opposite the place of the cavern
   They wrote the story on a column,

And on the great church window painted
The same, to make the world acquainted
How their children were stolen away,
And there it stands to this very day.
And I must not omit to say
That in Transylvania there's a tribe
Of alien people who ascribe
The outlandish ways and dress
On which their neighbors lay such stress,
To their fathers and mothers having risen
Out of some subterraneous prison
Into which they were trepanned
Long time ago in a mighty band
Out of Hamelin town in Brunswick land,
But how or why, they don't understand.

XV

So, Willy, let me and you be wipers
Of scores out with all men—especially pipers!
And, whether they pipe us free from rats or from mice,
If we've promised them aught, let us keep our promise!

–ROBERT BROWNING

A Visit from St. Nicholas

'Twas the night before Christmas, when all through the house
Not a creature was stirring, not even a mouse;
The stockings were hung by the chimney with care,
In hopes that St. Nicholas soon would be there;
The children were nestled all snug in their beds,
While visions of sugarplums danced in their heads;
And Mamma in her 'kerchief, and I in my cap,
Had just settled our brains for a long winter's nap—
When out on the lawn there arose such a clatter,
I sprang from my bed to see what was the matter.
Away to the window I flew like a flash,
Tore open the shutters, and threw up the sash.
The moon, on the breast of the new-fallen snow,
Gave the luster of midday to objects below;
When, what to my wondering eyes should appear,
But a miniature sleigh and eight tiny reindeer,
With a little old driver, so lively and quick,
I knew in a moment it must be St. Nick.
More rapid than eagles his coursers they came,
And he whistled, and shouted, and called them by name:
"Now, Dasher! now, Dancer! now, Prancer! and Vixen!
On, Comet! on, Cupid! on, Donder and Blitzen!
To the top of the porch! to the top of the wall!
Now dash away! dash away! dash away all!"
As dry leaves that before the wild hurricane fly,
When they meet with an obstacle, mount to the sky:
So up to the house-top the coursers they flew

Clement Moore, who was a professor of Greek and Oriental literature at a theological seminary in New York City, wanted to be known as a serious poet. Today he is remembered only for this poem, which he scribbled one winter evening to amuse his children.

With the sleigh full of toys, and St. Nicholas, too.
And then, in a twinkling, I heard on the roof
The prancing and pawing of each little hoof.
As I drew in my head, and was turning around,
Down the chimney St. Nicholas came with a bound.
He was dressed all in fur, from his head to his foot,
And his clothes were all tarnished with ashes and soot;
A bundle of toys he had flung on his back,
And he looked like a peddler just opening his pack.
His eyes—how they twinkled! his dimples, how merry!
His cheeks were like roses, his nose like a cherry!
His droll little mouth was drawn up like a bow,
And the beard on his chin was as white as the snow;
The stump of a pipe he held tight in his teeth,
And the smoke it encircled his head like a wreath;
He had a broad face, and a little round belly
That shook, when he laughed, like a bowl full of jelly.
He was chubby and plump, a right jolly old elf;
And I laughed when I saw him, in spite of myself.
A wink of his eye, and a twist of his head
Soon gave me to know I had nothing to dread.
He spoke not a word, but went straight to his work,
And he filled all the stockings; then turned with a jerk,
And laying his finger aside of his nose,
And giving a nod, up the chimney he rose.
He sprang to his sleigh, to his team gave a whistle,
And away they all flew like the down of a thistle.
But I heard him exclaim, ere he drove out of sight,
"Happy Christmas to all, and to all a good night!"

–CLEMENT MOORE

LET'S PRETEND

Fairies and witches, goblins and elves, giants and ogres, and
even a charming little ghost are among the wonderful characters
you'll meet in this enchanted land of Let's Pretend.

Dreams

Beyond, beyond the mountain line,
    The gray stone and the boulder,
Beyond the growth of dark green pine,
    That crowns its western shoulder,
There lies that fairy land of mine,
    Unseen of a beholder.

Its fruits are all like rubies rare,
    Its streams are clear as glasses:
There golden castles hang in air,
    And purple grapes in masses,
And noble knights and ladies fair
    Come riding down the passes.

Ah me! they say if I could stand
    Upon those mountain ledges,
I should but see on either hand
    Plain fields and dusty hedges:
And yet I know my fairy land
    Lies somewhere o'er their hedges.

—CECIL FRANCES ALEXANDER

In Fairyland

The fairy poet takes a sheet
      Of moonbeam, silver white;
His ink is dew from daisies sweet,
      His pen a point of light.

My love I know is fairer far
      Than his, (though she is fair,)
And we should dwell where fairies are—
      For I could praise her there.

–JOYCE KILMER

The Fairies

There are fairies at the bottom of our garden!
      It's not so very, very far away;
You pass the gardener's shed and you just keep straight ahead—
      I do so hope they've really come to stay.
There's a little wood, with moss in it and beetles,
      And a little stream that quietly runs through;
You wouldn't think they'd dare to come merry-making there—
      Well, they do.

There are fairies at the bottom of our garden!
      They often have a dance on summer nights;
The butterflies and bees make a lovely little breeze,
      And the rabbits stand about and hold the lights.

Did you know that they could sit upon the moonbeams
      And pick a little star to make a fan,
And dance away up there in the middle of the air?
        Well, they can.

There are fairies at the bottom of our garden!
      You cannot think how beautiful they are;
They all stand up and sing when the Fairy Queen and King
      Come gently floating down upon their car.
The King is very proud and very handsome;
      The Queen—now can you guess who that could be
(She's a little girl all day, but at night she steals away)?
      Well—it's me!

—ROSE FYLEMAN

The Castle in the Fire

The andirons were the dragons,
Set out to guard the gate
Of the old enchanted castle,
In the fire upon the grate.

We saw a turret window
Open a little space,
And frame, for just a moment,
A lady's lovely face:

Then, while we watched in wonder
From out the smoky veil,
A gallant knight came riding,
Dressed in coat of mail;

With slender lance a-tilting,
Thrusting with a skillful might,
He charged the crouching dragons—
Ah, 'twas a brilliant fight!

Then, in the roar and tumult,
The back log crashed in two,
And castle, knight, and dragons
Were hidden from our view;

But, when the smoke had lifted,
We saw, to our delight,
Riding away together,
The lady and the knight.

—MARY JANE CARR

The Little Elf

I met a little elf-man once,
Down where the lilies blow.
I asked him why he was so small
And why he didn't grow.

He slightly frowned, and with his eye
He looked me through and through.
"I'm quite as big for me," said he,
"As you are big for you."

–JOHN KENDRICK BANGS

John Kendrick Bangs, who was born in Yonkers, New York, was an editor of *Life* and *Harper's Magazine*. He wrote more than thirty volumes of humor and verse, and his poems and sketches were frequently published in children's magazines.

Catching Fairies

They're sleeping beneath the roses;
  Oh! kiss them before they rise,
And tickle their tiny noses,
    And sprinkle the dew on their eyes.
      Make haste, make haste;
      The fairies are caught;
        Make haste.

We'll put them in silver cages,
    And send them full-dress'd to court,
And maids of honor and pages
    Shall turn the poor things to sport.
      Be quick, be quick;
      Be quicker than thought;
        Be quick.

Their scarves shall be pennons for lancers,
    We'll tie up our flowers with their curls,
Their plumes will make fans for dancers,
    Their tears shall be set with pearls.
      Be wise, be wise;
      Make the most of the prize;
      Be wise.

They'll scatter sweet scents by winking,
    With sparks from under their feet;
They'll save us the trouble of thinking,
    Their voices will sound so sweet.
      Oh stay, oh stay:
      They're up and away:
      Oh stay!

—WILLIAM CORY

William Cory taught at Eton, the famous English public school. He wrote poetry for adults and children as well as a number of educational works.

The Butterfly's Ball

"Come, take up your hats, and away let us haste
To the Butterfly's Ball and the Grasshopper's Feast;
The trumpeter, Gadfly, has summoned the crew,
And the revels are now only waiting for you."

So said little Robert, and pacing along,
His merry companions came forth in a throng,
And on the smooth grass by the side of a wood,
Beneath a broad oak that for ages had stood,
Saw the children of earth and the tenants of air
For an evening's amusement together repair.

And there came the Beetle, so blind and so black,
Who carried the Emmet, his friend, on his back;
And there was the Gnat and the Dragonfly, too,
With all their relations, green, orange, and blue.

And there came the Moth, with his plumage of down,
And the Hornet, in jacket of yellow and brown,
Who with him the Wasp, his companion, did bring:
They promised that evening to lay by their sting.

And the sly little Dormouse crept out of his hold,
And brought to the feast his blind brother, the Mole.
And the Snail, with his horns peeping out of his shell,
Came from a great distance—the length of an ell.

A mushroom their table, and on it was laid
A water-dock leaf, which a tablecloth made.
The viands were various, to each of their taste,
And the Bee brought her honey to crown the repast.

William Roscoe, an Englishman, was a banker, writer, scholar, and book collector, in addition to being a poet. He published this amusing poem, "The Butterfly's Ball," in 1806 and it has become a children's classic.

Then close on his haunches, so solemn and wise,
The Frog from a corner looked up to the skies;
And the Squirrel, well-pleased such diversions to see,
Mounted high overhead and looked down from a tree.

Then out came a Spider, with fingers so fine,
To show his dexterity on the tight line.
From one branch to another his cobwebs he slung,
Then quick as an arrow he darted along.

But just in the middle—oh! shocking to tell,
From his rope, in an instant, poor Harlequin fell.
Yet he touched not the ground, but with talons outspread,
Hung suspended in air, at the end of a thread.

Then the Grasshopper came, with a jerk and a spring,
Very long was his leg, though but short was his wing;
He took but three leaps, and was soon out of sight,
Then chirped his own praises the rest of the night.

With step so majestic, the Snail did advance,
And promised the gazers a minuet to dance:
But they all laughed so loud that he pulled in his head,
And went to his own little chamber to bed.
Then as evening gave way to the shadows of night,
Their watchman, the Glow-worm, came out with a light.

"Then home let us hasten while yet we can see,
For no watchman is waiting for you and for me."
So said little Robert, and pacing along,
His merry companions returned in a throng.

–WILLIAM ROSCOE

The Plumpuppets

When little heads weary have gone to their bed,
When all the good nights and the prayers have been said,
Of all the good fairies that send bairns to rest
The little Plumpuppets are those I love best.

If your pillow is lumpy, or hot, thin, and flat,
The little Plumpuppets know just what they're at:
They plump up the pillow, all soft, cool, and fat—
       The little Plumpuppets plump-up it!

The little Plumpuppets are fairies of beds;
They have nothing to do but to watch sleepyheads;
They turn down the sheets and they tuck you in tight,
And they dance on your pillow to wish you good night!

–CHRISTOPHER MORLEY

The Unseen Playmate

When children are playing alone on the green
In comes the playmate that never was seen.
When children are happy and lonely and good,
The Friend of the Children comes out of the wood.

Nobody heard him and nobody saw,
His is a picture you never could draw,
But he's sure to be present, abroad or at home,
When children are happy and playing alone.

He lives in the laurels, he runs on the grass,
He sings when you tinkle the musical glass;
Whene'er you are happy and cannot tell why,
The Friend of the Children is sure to be by!

He loves to be little, he hates to be big,
'Tis he that inhabits the caves that you dig;
'Tis he when you play with your soldiers of tin
That sides with the Frenchmen and never can win.

'Tis he, when at night you go off to your bed,
Bids you go to your sleep and not trouble your head,
For wherever they're lying, in cupboard or shelf,
'Tis he will take care of your playthings himself!

–ROBERT LOUIS STEVENSON

The Sleepy Giant

My age is three hundred and seventy-two,
    And I think, with the deepest regret,
How I used to pick up and voraciously chew
    The dear little boys whom I met.

I've eaten them raw, in their holiday suits;
    I've eaten them curried with rice;
I've eaten them baked, in their jackets and boots,
    And found them exceedingly nice.

But now that my jaws are too weak for such fare,
    I think it exceeding rude
To do such a thing, when I'm quite well aware
    Little boys do not like to be chewed.

And so I contentedly live upon eels,
    And try to do nothing amiss,
And I pass all the time I can spare from my meals
    In innocent slumber—like this.

–CHARLES E. CARRYL

The Witches' Song

Thrice the brinded cat hath mew'd.
Thrice, and once the hedge pig whin'd.
Harper cries, "'Tis time, 'tis time."
Round about the cauldron go;
In the poison'd entrails throw.
Toad, that under cold stone
Days and nights has thirty-one
Swelter'd venom sleeping got,
Boil thou first i' the charmed pot.
      Double, double toil and trouble;
      Fire burn and cauldron bubble.

Fillet of a fenny snake,
In the cauldron boil and bake;
Eye of newt, and toe of frog,
Wool of bat, and tongue of dog,
Adder's fork, and blind-worm's sting,
Lizard's leg, and howler's wing,
For a charm of powerful trouble,
Like a hell-broth boil and bubble.
      Double, double toil and trouble;
      Fire burn and cauldron bubble.

—WILLIAM SHAKESPEARE

This most famous of witches' spells is from Act IV of William Shakespeare's play *Macbeth*.

The Dorchester Giant

There was a giant in times of old,
    A mighty one was he;
He had a wife, but she was a scold,
So he kept her shut in his mammoth fold;
    And he had children three.

It happened to be an election day,
    And the giants were choosing a king;
The people were not democrats then,
They did not talk of the rights of men,
    And all that sort of thing.

Then the giant took his children three,
    And fastened them in the pen;
The children roared; quoth the giant, "Be still!"
And Dorchester Heights and Milton Hill
    Rolled back the sound again.

Then he brought them a pudding stuffed with plums,
    As big as the State House dome;
Quoth he, "There's something for you to eat;
So stop your mouths with your 'lection treat,
    And wait till your dad comes home."

So the giant pulled him a chestnut stout,
    And whittled the boughs away;
The boys and their mother set up a shout,
Said he, "You're in and you can't get out,
    Bellow as loud as you may."

Oliver Wendell Holmes was born in Boston. He was a distinguished doctor as well as a world-renowned writer of poetry, essays, novels, and books on medical subjects. He got his medical degree at Harvard and for many years taught there. This amusing poem about a mighty giant is set in the Boston area, as anyone who lives there will realize.

Off he went, and he growled a tune
        As he strode the fields along;
'Tis said a buffalo fainted away,
And fell as cold as a lump of clay,
        When he heard the giant's song.

But whether the story's true or not,
        It isn't for me to show;
There's many a thing that's twice as queer
In somebody's lectures that we hear,
        And those are true you know.

What are those lone ones doing now,
        The wife and the children sad?
Oh, they are in a terrible rout,
Screaming, and throwing their pudding about,
        Acting as they were mad.

They flung it over to Roxbury hills,
        The flung it over the plain,
And all over Milton and Dorchester, too
Great lumps of pudding the giants threw;
        They tumbled as thick as rain.

Giant and mammoth have passed away,
        For ages have floated by;
The suet is hard as a marrowbone,
And every plum is turned to a stone,
        But there the puddings lie.

And if, some pleasant afternoon,
      You'll ask me out to ride,
The whole of the story I will tell,
And you shall see where the puddings fell,
      And pay for the punch beside.

–OLIVER WENDELL HOLMES

POEMS TO PONDER

The selections in this section are all poems that are good to think about.

One of them is about books, another is about music. There is a poem written

by Robert Frost, as well as poems by Rudyard Kipling and Emily Dickinson.

Read each of them slowly—and allow time to think and talk about it.

All Things Bright and Beautiful

All things bright and beautiful,
    All creatures great and small,
All things wise and wonderful,
    The Lord God made them all.

Each little flower that opens,
    Each little bird that sings,
He made their glowing colors,
    He made their tiny wings.

The purple-headed mountain,
    The river running by,
The sunset, and the morning,
    That brightens up the sky;

The cold wind in the winter,
    The pleasant summer sun,
The ripe fruits in the garden,
    He made them every one.

The tall trees in the greenwood,
    The meadows where we play,
The rushes by the water
    We gather every day—

He gave us eyes to see them,
    And lips that we might tell,
How great is God almighty,
    Who has made all things well.

—CECIL FRANCES ALEXANDER

This lovely poem first appeared in Cecil Frances Alexander's collection *Hymns for Little Children*, which she wrote in the mid-nineteenth century, before she was married and had children of her own.

The Bells

I

Hear the sledges with the bells—
Silver bells!
What a world of merriment their melody foretells!
How they tinkle, tinkle, tinkle,
In the icy air of night!
While the stars that oversprinkle
All the heavens, seem to twinkle
With a crystalline delight;
Keeping time, time, time,
In a sort of tunic rhyme,
To the tintinnabulation that so musically wells
From the bells, bells, bells, bells,
Bells, bells, bells—
From the jingling and the tinkling of the bells.

II

Hear the mellow wedding bells—
Golden bells!
What a world of happiness their harmony foretells!
Through the balmy air of night
How they ring out their delight!—
From the molten-golden notes,
And all in tune,
What a liquid ditty floats
To the turtledove that listens, while she gloats
On the moon!
Oh, from out the sounding cells,

What a gush of euphony voluminously wells!
How it swells!
How it dwells
On the Future!—how it tells
Of the rapture that impels
To the swinging and the ringing
Of the bells, bells, bells—
Of the bells, bells, bells, bells,
Bells, bells, bells—
To the rhyming and the chiming of the bells!

III

Hear the loud alarum bells—
Brazen bells!
What a tale of terror, now, their turbulency tells!
In the startled ear of night
How they scream out their affright!
Too much horrified to speak,
They can only shriek, shriek,
Out of tune,
In a clamorous appealing to the mercy of the fire,
In a mad expostulation with the deaf and frantic fire,
Leaping higher, higher, higher,
With a desperate desire,
And a resolute endeavor
Now—now to sit, or never,
By the side of the palefaced moon.
Oh, the bells, bells, bells!
What a tale their terror tells
Of Despair!

How they clang, and clash, and roar!
What a horror they outpour
On the bosom of the palpitating air!
Yet the ear, it fully knows,
By the twanging
And the clanging,
How the danger ebbs and flows;
Yet the ear distinctly tells,
In the jangling
And the wrangling,
How the danger sinks and swells,
By the sinking or the swelling in the anger of the
bells—
Of the bells,—
Of the bells, bells, bells, bells,
Bells, bells, bells—
In the clamor and the clangor of the bells!

IV
Hear the tolling of the bells—
Iron bells!
What a world of solemn thought their monody compels!
In the silence of the night,
How we shiver with affright
At the melancholy menace of their tone!
For every sound that floats
From the rust within their throats
Is a groan.
And the people—ah, the people—
They that dwell up in the steeple,

All alone,
And who tolling, tolling, tolling,
In that muffled monotone,
Feel a glory in so rolling
On the human heart a stone—
They are neither man nor woman—
They are neither brute nor human—
They are Ghools:
And their king it is who tolls:
And he rolls, rolls, rolls,
Rolls
A paean from the bells!
And his merry bosom swells
With the paean of the bells!
And he dances, and he yells;
Keeping time, time, time,
In a sort of Runic rhyme,
To the paean of the bells—
Of the bells:
Keeping time, time, time,
In a sort of Runic rhyme,
To the throbbing of the bells—
Of the bells, bells, bells—
To the sobbing of the bells;
Keeping time, time, time,
As he knells, knells, knells,
In a happy Runic rhyme,
To the rolling of the bells—
Of the bells, bells, bells:—
To the tolling of the bells—

Of the bells, bells, bells, bells,
Bells, bells, bells—
To the moaning and the groaning of the bells.

—EDGAR ALLAN POE

Precious Stones

An emerald is as green as grass,
  A ruby red as blood,
A sapphire shines as blue as heaven,
  But a flint lies in the mud.

A diamond is a brilliant stone
  To catch the world's desire,
An opal holds a rainbow light,
  But a flint holds fire.

—CHRISTINA ROSSETTI

If—

If you can keep your head when all about you
      Are losing theirs and blaming it on you;
If you can trust yourself when all men doubt you,
      But make allowance for their doubting too;
If you can wait and not be tired by waiting,
      Or, being lied about, don't deal in lies,
Or, being hated, don't give way to hating,
      And yet don't look too good, nor talk too wise;

If you can dream—and not make dreams your master;
      If you can think—and not make thoughts
      your aim;
If you can meet with triumph and disaster
      And treat those two imposters just the same;
If you can bear to hear the truth you've spoken
      Twisted by knaves to make a trap for fools,
Or watch the things you gave your life to, broken,
      And stoop and build 'em up with worn-out tools;

If you can make one heap of all your winnings
      And risk it on one turn of pitch-and-toss,
And lose, and start again at your beginnings
      And never breathe a word about your loss;
If you can force your heart and nerve and sinew
      To serve your turn long after they are gone,
And so hold on when there is nothing in you
      Except the Will which says to them: "Hold on!"

If you can talk with crowds and keep your virtue,
      Or walk with kings—nor lose the common touch;

Born in Bombay, India, Rudyard Kipling was sent to school in England when he was six years old. He returned to India eleven years later and began his career as a journalist, novelist, and poet. Generations of children have been delighted by the stories in his jungle books. "If—" is one of the most popular inspirational poems ever written. It is often seen framed in offices and schools and is frequently quoted on graduation cards.

If neither foes nor loving friends can hurt you;
      If all men count with you, but none too much;
If you can fill the unforgiving minute
      With sixty seconds' worth of distance run—
Yours is the Earth and everything that's in it,
      And—which is more—you'll be a Man, my son!

–RUDYARD KIPLING

Hope

"Hope" is the thing with feathers
That perches in the soul,
And sings the tune without the words,
And never stops at all,

And sweetest in the gale is heard;
And sore must be the storm
That could abash the little bird
That keeps so many warm.

I've heard it in the chillest land,
And on the strangest sea;
Yet, never, in extremity,
It asked a crumb of me.

–EMILY DICKINSON

What is Pink?

What is pink? A rose is pink
By the fountain's brink.
What is red? A poppy's red
In its barley bed.
What is blue? The sky is blue
Where the clouds float through.
What is white? A swan is white
Sailing in the light.
What is yellow? Pears are yellow,
Rich and ripe and mellow.
What is green? The grass is green,
With small flowers between.
What is violet? Clouds are violet
In the summer twilight.
What is orange? Why, an orange,
Just an orange!

–CHRISTINA ROSSETTI

There is No Frigate Like a Book

There is no frigate like a book
      To take us lands away,
Nor any coursers like a page
      Of prancing poetry.
This traverse may the poorest take
      without oppress of toll;
How frugal is the chariot
      That bears a human soul!

–EMILY DICKINSON

Abou Ben Adhem

Abou Ben Adhem (may his tribe increase!)
Awoke one night from a deep dream of peace,
And saw, within the moonlight in his room,
Making it rich, and like a lily in bloom,
An angel writing in a book of gold:
Exceeding peace had made Ben Adhem bold,
And to the Presence in the room he said,
"What writest thou?" The vision raised its head,
And with a look made of all sweet accord
Answered, "The names of those who love the Lord."
"And is mine one?" said Abou. "Nay, not so,"
Replied the angel. Abou spoke more low,
But cheerily still; and said, "I pray thee, then,
Write me as one that loves his fellow men."

The angel wrote, and vanished. The next night
It came again with a great wakening light,
And showed the names whom love of God had blessed,
And, lo! Ben Adhem's name led all the rest.

–LEIGH HUNT

Leigh Hunt did not actually write this poem. It is his translation of a French poem based on an Islamic legend that tells how Allah, on the night of a particular feast day, checks in a golden book the names of those who love him.

The Road Not Taken

Two roads diverged in a yellow wood,
And sorry I could not travel both
And by one traveler, long I stood
And looked down one as far as I could
To where it bent in the undergrowth;

Then took the other, as just as fair,
And having perhaps the better claim,
Because it was grassy and wanted wear;
Though as for that, the passing there
Had worn them really about the same,

And both that morning equally lay
In leaves no step had trodden black.
Oh, I kept the first for another day!
Yet knowing how way leads on to way,
I doubted if I should ever come back.

I shall be telling this with a sigh
Somewhere ages and ages hence:
Two roads diverged in a wood, and I—
I took the one less traveled by,
And that has made all the difference.

−ROBERT FROST

Born in San Francisco, Robert Frost settled permanently on a farm in New Hampshire after several jobs as a laborer and a period of farming in New England. He never graduated from college, but he won twenty-five honorary degrees, and was the only poet to receive four Pulitzer Prizes. He said that he wrote this poem almost effortlessly one morning after staying up all night to work on a long poem. It was his favorite poem. He called it "my best bid for remembrance."

Sea Fever

I must go down to the seas again, to the lonely sea and the sky,
And all I ask is a tall ship and a star to steer her by;
And the wheel's kick and the wind's song and the white sail's
      shaking,
And a gray mist on the sea's face, and a gray dawn breaking.

I must go down to the seas again, for call of the running
        tide
Is a wild call and a clear call that may not be denied;
And all I ask is a windy day with the white clouds flying,
And the flung spray and the blown spume, and the sea gulls
      crying.

I must go down to the seas again, to the vagrant gypsy life,
To the gull's way and the whale's way where the wind's like
      a whetted knife;
And all I ask is a merry yarn from a laughing fellow-rover,
And quiet sleep and a sweet dream when the long trick's over.

—JOHN MASEFIELD

John Masefield, who was born in England, served as a merchant seaman in the age of sailing ships. He jumped ship for various jobs in New York and London until he began to tell wonderful tales of the sea in prose and in poetry. "Sea Fever" is one of his most popular poems.

Music

The neighbor sits in his window and plays the flute.
From my bed I can hear him,
And the round notes flutter and tap about the room,
And hit against each other,
Blurring to unexpected chords.
It is very beautiful,
With the little flute-notes all about me,
In the darkness.

In the daytime,
The neighbor eats bread and onions with one hand
And copies music with the other.
He is fat and has a bald head,
So I do not look at him,
But run quickly past his window.
There is always the sky to look at,
Or the water in the well!

But when night comes and he plays his flute,
I think of him as a young man,
With gold seals hanging from his watch,
And a blue coat with silver buttons.
As I lie in my bed
The flute-notes push against my ears and lips.
And I go to sleep, dreaming.

—AMY LOWELL

Amy Lowell was born in Brookline, Massachusetts, into a wealthy and prominent New England family. She was one of the first so called imagist poets in the United States, breaking with tradition and writing poems that did not rhyme and were about any subject the writer chose. She went on lecture and reading tours and with her enormous enthusiasm and theatrical presence she excited audiences and was successful in bringing American poetry into the twentieth century.

Caged Bird

A free bird leaps
on the back of the wind
and floats downstream
till the current ends
and dips his wing
in the orange sun rays
and dares to claim the sky.

But a bird that stalks
down his narrow cage
can seldom see through
his bars of rage
his wings are clipped and
his feet are tied
so he opens his throat to sing.

The caged bird sings
with a fearful trill
of things unknown
but longed for still
and his tune is heard
on the distant hill
for the caged bird
sings of freedom.

The free bird thinks of another breeze
and the trade winds soft through the sighing trees
and the fat worms waiting on a dawn-bright lawn
and he names the sky his own.

But a caged bird stands on the grave of dreams
his shadow shouts on a nightmare scream
his wings are clipped and his feet are tied
so he opens his throat to sing.

The caged bird sings
with a fearful trill
of things unknown
but longed for still
and his tune is heard
on the distant hill
for the caged bird
sings of freedom.

–MAYA ANGELOU

List of Illustrators

Fanny Y. Cory
Marguerite Davis
Kate Greenway
Jessie Willcox Smith

Index